PREACHING
CHRIST

PREACHING CHRIST

*An Address to
Those Entering the
Christian Ministry*

Charles P. McIlvaine

THE BANNER OF TRUTH TRUST

THE BANNER OF TRUTH TRUST
3 Murrayfield Road, Edinburgh EH12 6EL, UK
P O Box 621, Carlisle, PA 17013, USA

*

© Banner of Truth 2003
ISBN 0 85151 831 1

*

First published 1863
First Banner of Truth edition 2003

*

Typeset in 13/18 pt Centaur at
the Banner of Truth Trust
Printed in Great Britain by
Bell & Bain Ltd.,
Glasgow

❧ Contents ❧

✆ Publisher's Foreword ☙

The Rt. Rev. Charles Pettit McIlvaine (1799–1873) was the son of a U.S. Senator from New Jersey and nephew of a Pennsylvania Governor. He was born in Burlington, New Jersey, on 18 January 1799 and received his early education at Burlington Academy, before attending Princeton College, from which he graduated in 1816.

In 1815 the College experienced a powerful religious revival.[1] Recalling the events of that year in later life, McIlvaine said:

> It is more than forty years since I first witnessed a revival of religion. It was in the college of which I was a student. It was powerful and pervading, and fruitful in the conversion of

[1] See Iain H. Murray, *Revival and Revivalism* (Edinburgh: Banner of Truth, 1994), pp. 136–7, 141; and David B. Calhoun, *Princeton Seminary: Faith and Learning, 1812–68* (Edinburgh: Banner of Truth, 1994), pp. 79–80.

young men to God . . . In that precious season of the power of God, my religious life began. I had *heard* before; I then began to *know*. I must doubt the deepest convictions of my soul, when I doubt whether that revival was the work of the Spirit of God.[1]

On graduating from Princeton, McIlvaine felt called to minister in the Episcopal church, the church of his childhood, and was ordained a deacon in 1820. He became rector of a church in Washington D.C. and was made a chaplain to the Senate while still in his early twenties. Shortly afterwards he was appointed chaplain at West Point Military Academy. While at West Point he was instrumental in a revival among the cadets there.

In all his appointments in the Episcopal church, McIlvaine sought to counter the prevailing 'high-church' attitudes in the denomination and to shift the emphasis from ceremony and ritual to Scripture and personal salvation. His question to his ordinands was, 'Have you fled to Christ and committed your soul to him as all your refuge and righteousness?'

In 1832 he accepted a call from the Diocese of Ohio to become Bishop and soon began to reorganize Kenyon College in Gambier, Ohio, and its associated seminary, travelling to England to raise money for the seminary.

[1] Quoted in Heman Humphrey, *Revival Sketches and Manual* (New York, 1859), p. 94. See also Iain H. Murray, *Revival and Revivalism*, p. 141.

As Bishop of Ohio, McIlvaine proved a dynamic leader, preaching often, establishing parishes, supervising Kenyon College, writing theological papers and co-operating in gospel endeavours with Presbyterians and Methodists. He drew the line in co-operation, however, at the type of revivalism represented by Charles Finney. In this form of Protestantism he saw 'the spirit of reckless innovation, contemptuous insubordination, formal fanaticism and fanatical informality'.

Already a prominent churchman and educator, McIlvaine also served his country as a diplomat. While in England in late 1861, at the request of President Lincoln and Secretary of State William Seward, he presented the Lincoln administration's case against recognizing the Confederacy to the British government.

He died in Florence, Italy, on 14 March 1873. While being transported back to the United States, his body lay in state in Westminster Abbey for four days. A ceremony was held in the central aisle to honour his memory. The only other American citizen who has been honoured in this way is Sir Winston Churchill.

Preaching Christ was originally a charge delivered to the clergy of the Diocese of Ohio at their annual convention in Akron, Ohio, in June 1863 and published in New York soon afterwards. Evidently feeling that his ministry was drawing to a close, he described his topic as 'a subject with which a

Bishop may well choose to close his ministry, which indeed all our work should be identified with, and which, I am thankful to say, has been obtaining, ever since mine began, a deeper and stronger possession of my mind, my affections and my ministry – I mean *the work of preaching Christ,* according to the Scriptures, and the example of the Apostles'.

As an Appendix we have added an example of the effective preaching of Christ, the first sermon preached by C. H. Spurgeon in the newly-opened Metropolitan Tabernacle, London, in 1861.

May the republication of McIlvaine's exhortation in this form promote the great work of preaching Christ in an age which stands in as great a need as any age before it of the truth of 'Jesus Christ and him crucified'.

THE PUBLISHER
January 2003

I

⟡

How Did the Apostles Preach Christ?

My Dear Brother in Christ,

You have been pursuing an education of mind and heart, preparatory to the office of a minister of the gospel. You are now upon the threshold of that sacred work. How far your ministry will be that of a faithful 'steward of the mysteries of God' will depend on how far it shall be the faithful preaching of Jesus Christ. No inquiry, therefore, in the course of your preparation, or at this stage of your career, should seem to you of such importance as that which seeks a full understanding of the work of preaching Christ Jesus our Lord and Saviour, according as it is taught in the Scriptures and set before us in the example of the Apostles. It is an inquiry with which the work of a minister of Christ will be more and more identified as he himself shall grow in the mind of his Master, and in a personal experience of the power and preciousness of the grace revealed in him.

It is now forty years since I was called of God, and in his Providence permitted and enabled to take part in this holy ministry. More and more have I learned the need that ministers should keep their teaching close to that one central and living theme, if they would have it honoured of God as his power unto salvation. And the need also of constant and jealous watchfulness against the many snares and by-ways by which we may be led into such departures therefrom as will have the effect in part, if not entirely, of unevangelizing our work.

Allow me therefore, out of an earnest desire to promote your usefulness and happiness in the office to which you trust you are inwardly called by the Holy Ghost, to request your serious and prayerful attention to these pages, addressed to you by one whose age and experience of these things are his title to speak to you on such subjects.

I propose to you, as our starting-point, the question, *What is embraced in the work of preaching Christ according to the mind of the Spirit, as exhibited in the teaching of his Word, and in the practice of his Apostles?*

'Go . . . preach the gospel' were the words of our Lord to his Apostles, which conveyed to them and to us the whole weight and substance of the commission of his ministers and ambassadors. It was the unquestioning obedience of a simple and unhesitating faith to that one command, animated by an unquenchable love to its divine Author and to the souls he died to save, enlightened by the teaching and made mighty by the power of the Holy Ghost, that constituted all the vigour and efficacy of the ministry of the Apostles.

It was thus that their weapons of warfare became 'mighty through God', and achieved those stupendous victories of the truth over 'the spirit that worketh in the children of disobedience', which the weaker faith and more timid obedience of the church in later days have so poorly imitated. And as in the beginning, so also in all times of the Christian dispensation, it has pleased God that sinners shall be brought 'into captivity to the obedience of Christ', and made partakers of his salvation, by the obedience of his ministers to that one original charge and command, *'Preach the gospel'.* Faith by hearing, gospel faith by hearing gospel truth, and such hearing by the preaching of the Word of God, is his standing rule according to which he bestows his Spirit for the conviction, conversion and sanctification of men.

But it is manifest from the Scriptures that the Apostles identified the gospel *with Christ;* so that, in their view and practice, to preach the gospel was neither more nor less than to preach Christ. The record which, in a few words, describes their ministry is, that, 'daily in the temple and in every house they ceased not to teach and preach Jesus Christ'. St Paul writing to the Romans defines the whole gospel by saying that it is 'concerning Jesus Christ' (*Rom.* 1:3). The employment of his two years' imprisonment at Rome was all comprehended in 'teaching those things which concern the Lord Jesus Christ'. And his whole ministry was given unto him, he testifies, that he 'might preach the unsearchable riches of Christ'. As he could say, 'For me to live is Christ', so for him to *preach* was Christ. To him Christ and the gospel were one.

But we must here note the chief feature in their preaching of Christ. They omitted nothing pertaining to him; but there was one thing on which, more than anything else, they very particularly and emphatically dwelt. They took great pains to set forth the Lord Jesus in all that he was and is; in Person and office, as once on earth, and now in heaven; his pre-existent glory with the Father, his incarnation and humiliation in our nature, his death, resurrection, and intercession; all his love, all his promises, all his commandments; so that there was no part of the whole counsel of God 'concerning his Son Jesus Christ' which they kept back. But manifestly there was one event in his history, one work amidst all his works, which stood in their view as *the* great event and work, around which they gathered the force of their testimony, as its central light and power – to which they made all that went before it look forward for consummation, and all that succeeded it look back as to its foundation, and on the faithful declaration of which, with its immediate connections, they very especially rested the faithfulness of their work as preachers of the gospel.

No doubt you anticipate me. Such passages of the Apostles arise to your minds, as, 'We preach Christ *crucified*'; 'I determined not to know anything among you (while declaring unto you the testimony of God) save Jesus Christ and him *crucified*'; 'God forbid that I should glory save in the *cross* of our Lord Jesus Christ'; 'For the preaching of the cross is to them that perish foolishness, but unto us which are saved it is the power of God.' They preached Christ – but as *Christ crucified*.

They said continually, like John the Baptist, 'Behold the Lamb of God, which taketh away the sin of the world', but it was the 'Lamb *slain*' – Christ *in his death* – bearing 'our sins in his own body on the tree', that they pointed to. They rejoiced in everything pertaining to their Lord, from his birth at Bethlehem to his present glory at the Father's right hand, but the one thing in which they rejoiced so supremely was his cross.

Of the two sacraments ordained of Christ for his church, that which alone goes with the believer, to be renewed and repeated all along the way of his earthly life, has for its great object to 'show the Lord's *death* until he come'. It was a great lesson which the Lord thus taught us as to how we must preach him. His Apostles therefore became in speech what that sacrament is in symbol, constantly showing the Lord's death as the sinner's life. Thus, when they spoke of the Christian's race for 'the prize of the high calling of God in Christ Jesus' – and when they exhorted us while in that contest to be always 'looking unto Jesus' – the special aspect in which they presented him was as *enduring the cross*.

And I need not here say that their sense of the supreme importance in their ministry of the death of Christ was because they beheld therein the one only and the one all-sufficient sacrifice and propitiation, the *vicarious* atonement, for the sins of the whole world; that great work of God wherein he laid in Zion for a sure foundation, the precious cornerstone, on which the sinner believing shall not be confounded. It is all contained in one verse – 'Christ hath once suffered for sins, the just for the unjust, to bring us to God' (*I Pet.* 3:18). And again, 'Christ hath redeemed us from the curse of the law, being made a curse for us' (*Gal.* 3:13).

Thus we have our lesson and example. In the way the Apostles preached the gospel we must try to preach it. As they preached Christ, so must we. God forbid that we should glory in anything else as ministers of the Word. Preachers of Christ, according to the mind of Christ – ah, how all honours, all satisfaction in our work, will perish but that! When our stewardship is to be accounted for, and we are just departing, and the veil, half drawn aside, discloses what we are to meet and what to be forever, how then shall we care for praise of learning, or praise of speech, or any vapours of men's applause! But then, to have 'the testimony of our conscience that in simplicity and godly sincerity, not with enticing words of man's wisdom', we have made it our life-business and our heart-pleasure to 'teach and preach Jesus Christ', as they did whom he gave to be our examples, having ourselves first learned his preciousness to our own souls, oh, what consolation and thankfulness with which to die!

Evidently then, my brethren, it is a most serious question to be always studying, how we may so proclaim the truth committed to us in Holy Scripture, that in the sense of the Apostles it may be said of us in our whole ministry, that 'we preach *Christ crucified*'. To this we devote this address.

2

⌘

How Some Fail
in Preaching
Christ

Many are the failures, many the egregious failures,
in preaching Christ. Sometimes it seems as if the
preacher could preach just as he does if Christ and his work
were a mere incident in religion, a name, and little more —
answering now and then as a convenience to a sentence;
introduced occasionally, because, under some texts, it is not
easily avoided, but never as the root and foundation out of
which our whole ministry proceeds. But what awful
condemnation to be thus essentially defective at the very heart

of the great work committed to us! Nothing can in the least atone for it. You might as well attempt to turn night into day by lighting a candle as a substitute for the sun. Our ministry is all darkness, emptiness, and powerlessness; all condemnation to us, all delusion to those who hear us, all dishonour to the grace of God, whatever the breath of man may say of it, except as it is pervaded, illumined, filled with the testimony of Christ as once the sacrifice for sin, crucified and slain, now the glorified and ever-living Intercessor for all that come unto God by him.

There are many ways of approaching more or less to that attainment without ever reaching it. Some of the most common we will endeavour to state.

๑ Religious Truth Not Enough ๑

It is very possible to preach a great deal of important religious truth, and so that there shall be no admixture of important error in doctrine or precept – yea, truth having an important relation to Christ and his office – and yet not to preach Christ. The defect will be, not in the presence of what should not be there, but in the absence of that which is necessary to give all the truth delivered the character of 'truth as it is in Jesus'. Such absence, when nevertheless all is true, may be more destructive to the gospel character of the preaching than even the introduction of some positive error. The preaching may be very earnest. It may contain much that is affecting and deeply impressive – strong emotions may be stirred in the hearers. The earnest inquiry may be excited, What must we do? And yet the preaching may wholly fail in giving any such distinct answer to that question as will turn the attention of the inquirer to Christ as all his refuge. You may say a great deal about and around the gospel, and never preach the gospel.

Religious truths are not the gospel, except in proportion as, like John the Baptist, they point to the Lamb of God. For example, suppose you preach on the vanity of the world; the uncertainty of life; the awfulness of death unprepared for; the tremendous events of the judgment-day; the little profit of gaining the whole world and losing the soul; suppose you enlarge on the necessity and blessedness of a religious life, and the happiness of the saved. Does it follow that you have preached the gospel, or any part of it? If deep impressions are made, and serious inquiries excited, does it follow that Christ is preached?

Such topics unquestionably belong most legitimately to our ministry; they are important parts of the truth given us to enforce; but they are entirely subordinate and preliminary. They are not the distinctive *seed* of the word from which God has ordained that newness of life shall spring. They are rather the plough and the harrow to open and stir the ground, that it may receive the seed of life.

You may spend all your time in such work – not omitting to sprinkle your discourses with the oft-repeated name of Christ and with much gospel language; and just because there is no pervading exhibition of Christ, in his work of justification by his righteousness, and of sanctification by his Spirit, given so pointedly and plainly that whosoever will may understand, you may never attain to the honour, in the sight of God, of teaching and preaching Jesus Christ.

Nor is it sufficient that you may be reckoned to have done so by those who have not learned to discriminate between truth that is *religious,* and truth that is not only religious, but distinctively *gospel*-truth; who know not the difference between such preaching as makes the hearer feel some spiritual want, and that which also tells him what he wants, and where and how he is to find it.

The hearer who has learned Christ as his lesson of heart and life, of hope and peace, and knows nothing as precious to his soul, but as it leads him to Jesus on the cross of sacrifice, and on the throne of intercession, Jesus in his invitations and promises, Jesus in his grace to help, his righteousness to justify, and his power to sanctify, will feel that in all that ministry *'one thing is needful'*. That one thing, the very thing on which all its gospel character hinges, is CHRIST.

♔ Preaching Duty According to the ♔ Law Not Enough

But let us advance a little farther. You may preach with faithfulness and plainness the strictness and holiness of the law, how it enters with its requirements into the thoughts and affections of the heart, pronouncing condemnation on the sinner, and bringing us all in guilty before God. There may be no shrinking from the fullest exposition of the Scriptures concerning the end of the impenitent; no lack of earnest calls to repentance, nor of solemn declarations of the necessity of a new heart, and of holiness if we would see the Lord.

Still more: the office of Christ as the only Saviour, and his merits as the only plea, may be introduced not unfrequently, and yet may there be a great lack of such distinct holding up of Christ crucified, as Moses lifted up the serpent in the wilderness before the dying Israelites for all to see and live – such presentation of God's great remedy for every man's necessities as belongs to the consistency, simplicity, and fullness of the work committed to the minister of the gospel.

While speaking much of duty, the grace to enable us to do it may not be proportionably presented. While the need of personal holiness, and of a new heart as its essential basis, may be strongly urged, you may keep almost entirely out of sight the work of the Spirit of life in Christ Jesus, from whom all holy desires and all newness of heart and life proceed.

While the penalties of sin may be kept in full view, the fullness, and tenderness, and earnestness of the invitations and promises of Christ to the sinner turning unto God may be very dimly exhibited.

That great lesson, which we have need to be always studying, may have been but little learned – how to preach the law as showing our need of the righteousness of Christ, and how to preach the gospel as establishing and honouring the law; the one to convince of sin and condemnation, the other as providing a deliverance so complete that to the believer there is no condemnation; the one as taking away all pleas derived from ourselves, the other as furnishing a most perfect and prevailing plea in the mediation of Christ; the law as giving the rule of life, the gospel as giving the power of life, yea, life from death, in Jesus Christ; the law to humble us under a consciousness of an utter beggary before God, the gospel as directing us to him in whom it pleased the Father that all fullness should dwell.

ᑌ Truths Concerning Christ ᑌ Not Enough

Again, it may be that doctrine immediately concerning the Lord Jesus, and bringing his Person and office into view, may be much introduced. We may take opportunity to speak of the infinite dignity of his being; the mystery of his incarnation; the humiliation and love and grace of his coming in our nature; his tenderness, and compassion, and power to save; the perfectness of his example, and the depth of his sufferings.

Indeed, everything revealed concerning him may at times be found in our teaching, without error, and in each particular, as it stands by itself, without serious defect. But there may be still an important deficiency. The *proportion of truth* may not be kept. There is a proportion of parts in the whole body of gospel truth just as in our own bodies. We must omit none of the parts, but put each in its right relation to all the rest. To fail in this, so that, while we embrace all, we deform all by a disproportionate exaltation of some and depression of others, may be just as destructive of the gospel character of our ministry, just as confusing and misleading, as if we omitted some truths and perverted others.

For example, you may preach Christ in various aspects; but Christ *crucified*, the great Sacrifice of propitiation, though not omitted, may not have that high place, that central place, that all-controlling place, that place of the head-stone of the corner, which is necessary to its right adjustment to all parts of the system of faith. You may preach the incarnation of Christ in all its truth as a separate event, and yet in great error as regards its relation to other events, making it so unduly prominent that his death shall be made to appear comparatively subordinate and unessential, the means exalted above the end, the preparation of the body of Christ for sacrifice being made of more importance and more effective in our salvation, than his offering of that body on the cross.

But the Sacrament of the Lord's Supper, which we carry with us all the way of our journey, as our great confession, and joy, and glory, was appointed to show, as oft as we eat that bread and drink that cup, not the Lord's *birth*, or life, but 'the Lord's *death* until he come'.

You may preach all of Christ's work as well as his Person, and all in due proportion of parts, and yet some other vital truth essentially connected, may be so disproportionately presented as to create in the whole a most important defect. You have exhibited the foundation which God hath laid in Zion. The question remains, how the sinner is to avail himself of that foundation. He is to build thereon. But how? The Apostle answers, '*He that believeth* on him shall not be confounded.' We build *by faith*. We cannot preach Christ without preaching on that by which we become 'partakers of Christ'. Confusion, indistinctness, feebleness, deficiency there, must produce the same effect throughout the whole gospel.

If faith, in its nature, office, efficacy, and distinctive operation and fruits, be kept in a place so obscure, so subordinate, or taught so confusedly, that either it is wholly out of sight or hid in a crowd of other things, placed in the outer court of the temple instead of immediately by the altar of sacrifice, as the one instrumental grace by which the sinner partakes of the 'Lamb of God'; if the works which are its fruits, be so confounded with itself that the grace by which we are 'rooted and grounded' in Christ is made of no more influence in our participation of him than the several works of righteousness which grow out of its life, and follow upon the participation of Christ through its agency – then is the relative adjustment of truth most seriously spoiled and deformed.

⁓ Occasional Preaching of Christ ⁓ Not Enough

Further, under this head of our inquiry, it may be that occasionally in a discourse, now and then, the setting forth of Christ is satisfactory in point of doctrine, and the proportion of truth. But it may be only occasionally thus, and only when the text so obliges, according to rhetorical propriety, that we cannot avoid it. But such texts may not be chosen very often. Passing from subject to subject, the preacher comes, from time to time, to one which leads to the manifestation of Christ, in some leading feature of his grace and salvation; and then all may be well done, and calculated to enlighten a mind hungering for the truth.

But, meanwhile, you may hear many a discourse which contains scarcely more of anything distinctive of the gospel, or pertaining to Christ, except perhaps his name sometimes introduced, than if it were some other religion than Christ's of which the preacher is the minister.

And in the general course of his work, we may look in vain after such evident fondness of heart for views which most intimately and directly look *unto Jesus;* such habitual feeding of the flock in pastures watered by the river that proceedeth out of the throne of God and the Lamb; such strong tendency, when subjects not directly testifying of Christ must be handled, to keep them as near to him as possible, and to return from them as soon as possible to others of a nearer neighbourhood to the cross; such desire to illuminate all subjects with light from 'the face of Jesus Christ' as proves the preacher's determination 'to know nothing among men but Jesus Christ and him crucified'.

In the ministrations of such a preacher as we have in mind we miss that *habitualness* of the testimony of Christ, that special love for all the region round about Gethsemane and Calvary, the atonement and the intercession, and the great gifts of the Spirit purchased thereby; we miss that constant tracing of all spiritual life and consolation in its every influence and fruit, to Christ as the life, and that careful binding of all spiritual affections and duties upon him for support and strength, as the vine-dresser trains his vine upon its trellis, which appears so remarkably in the teaching of the Apostles.

❧ Preaching Christ 'with Wisdom ❧ of Words' Not Enough

Lastly, there is a way of preaching, which, in a dry, *doctrinal* sense, may avoid all the defects we have adverted to, and yet in a very serious measure include them all. It seems to be formed on the idea that it is inapplicable, in these days of advancement, to preach the simple gospel in its own *simplicity*, surrounding and setting forth its truths with scriptural illustrations and associations, so that it shall be not only the gospel in the substance of its doctrine, but the gospel in its nature, form, visage, drapery, and savour.

The idea of the preacher seems to be that such preaching would be considered antiquated and worn out; something requiring more originality, more depth of philosophical investigation, is demanded, to make people hear the gospel. You must make it look as little like the gospel as is consistent with preserving substantially the gospel doctrine.

The preacher preaches *himself.* To make the hearer regard him as a man of thought and depth, elevated by education above that simplicity of teaching which he supposes anybody can attain to, he affects the philosopher, deals in abstractions, dissociates the Master's message from the authority and mind of the Master and the simplicity of his inspired Word; as if the *wise* only, such as are capable of appreciating great efforts of mind, were expected to understand.

He seeks to use a 'wisdom of words' which St Paul rejected, 'lest the cross of Christ should be made of none effect'. To prevent the preaching of the cross from being 'foolishness' to the natural man, who 'receiveth not the things of the Spirit of God . . . because they are spiritually discerned', he so departs from the preaching of the cross as St Paul gave it that his preaching is not, and cannot expect to be, *'in demonstration of the Spirit and of power'*.

They that hear to be pleased with a show of mind are perhaps gratified. They that come to be elevated in their affections to things above, and to be fed with the bread of heaven, are sorely disappointed. They came to see *Jesus*. They have seen only that man in the pulpit and his empty abstractions. They asked bread, and he gave them a stone. There is much of such wretched work in various degrees; and some people have become, in their appetite, so *reduced* to it, that if a minister be not of that sort, they turn away from him, as one who is not *deep* enough for their minds. Away with such chaff, in view of the day when 'the fire shall try every man's work of what sort it is'.

We have thus endeavoured to indicate some of the paths by which, without delivering anything untrue, and while delivering much important truth, we may come short of the duty under consideration. We proceed to consider how we may fulfil it.

3

❦

WHAT IS IT
TO PREACH
CHRIST?

We have a great example in our Lord's own teaching. When, after his resurrection, he met the two disciples on the way to Emmaus, and found them in such darkness and doubt concerning himself, it is written that, 'beginning at Moses, and all the prophets, he expounded unto them, in all the Scriptures, the things concerning himself' – *the things concerning himself*. The office of the ministry is so to expound the Scriptures in all their parts as bring out the things concerning that glorious One, *himself*. St Paul therefore said that he was 'separated unto the gospel of God

. . . concerning his Son Jesus Christ' (*Rom.* 1:1–3). To teach
sinners to know Christ, and to 'count all things but loss for
the excellency of the knowledge of him', looking to the power
of the Holy Ghost to communicate through the truth, which
we give only in the letter, that spiritual and saving knowledge
which only God giveth, is the general expression of our duty.

But in the gospel 'concerning our Lord Jesus Christ', that
is, in the circle of doctrines and duties and promises and
blessings which constitute the message of great salvation in
him, there is, as we have already hinted, a system of parts
mutually related and dependent, all in perfect harmony, none
so obscure or remote as to be of no importance to the right
representation of the whole. That system, like that of our sun,
has a centre, by which all the parts are held in place, from
which all their light and life proceed, and around which all
revolve. You cannot exhibit the system of truth and duty till
you have made known that central light and power; nor can
you make known that power in all its truth without exhibiting
those surrounding and dependent parts of doctrine and
precept.

That central sun of light and life is Christ. All of gospel
truth and duty, of consolation and strength, abides in Christ
– derives from Christ, and glorifies Christ – and must be so
presented, or else it is divorced from its only life, and loses its
gospel character. He is the True Vine, and all parts of gospel
truth are branches in him. Let such truth be presented

without that connection, then its character as truth may remain, but its character for '*truth as it is in Jesus*' is lost. Its vitality is gone. Fruit of life in Christ Jesus it cannot produce. It is just as true and important concerning religious truth as concerning religious men, that 'the branch cannot bring forth fruit except it abide in the vine'.

ᴥ Begin with Christ ᴥ

Now, what is the best mode of setting forth this system of grace? Where shall we begin? Shall we first take up the elements of religion, the outsides of the circle; reasoning upward from general truths to the more particular; explaining and enforcing ordinances and institutions of the church as our road of approach to the Head and Life of the church; confining attention to means of grace before we have directed our hearers to the grace itself in the great Fountain-head; and thus gradually, and after a long process of preparatory work, arrive at last at the Person, and mission, and sacrifice of Christ? But we must remember who they are whom we are thus keeping so long in the cold and in the dark. They are sinners under the condemnation of the law of God. They are dying sinners. How brief the time of some of them to learn, you know not. You have no time to spend on preliminaries before you have introduced them to the great salvation. What they have most need to know is, he who came to seek and to save the lost – how they may find him, and what are the terms of his salvation.

Begin at once with Christ – 'Behold the Lamb of God' is the voice. There is no light till that Light appears. The icy bondage of the sinner's heart yields not till that Sun is risen. Astronomers, when they teach the solar system, begin with the sun. Thence to the related and dependent orbits is easy. So the Apostles taught. See how, when they had the whole system of the gospel, as distinguished from that of the law, to teach the Jews – the whole outward and visible of the Christian Church, as well as all the inward and spiritual of the Christian life, all so new, and strange, and unpalatable to a people so unprepared, so entangled with traditionary aversions and deep-seated perversions, see how they leaped over all preliminaries, and began at once with Christ and him crucified, the sacrifice of his death, and 'the power of his resurrection'. At once they broke ground and set up the banner of their ministry there.

Just at the point where the pride of the sinner would most revolt, and the wisdom of man was most at fault, and the ignorance of Jew and Gentile was most complete, where the Jew saw only a stumbling-block and the Greek only foolishness, there they opened their message. 'I delivered unto you, *first of all*', said St Paul, 'that which I also received, how that Christ died for our sins, according to the Scriptures' (*I Cor.* 15:3). They could not wait to root out prejudice, plant first principles, approach the intrenched power 'that worketh in the children of disobedience' by the strategy of man's wisdom, when they knew that Christ was the great 'power of God unto salvation'.

At once to open the windows and let in the sun was their way of giving light to them that sat in darkness. At once to show the amazing love of God to sinners in not sparing his own Son but delivering him up for us all was their way to draw the sinner's heart to God. Human device would have said, as it has often said, in substance, Make philosophy prepare the way. Clothe your teaching in robes of man's wisdom. Keep back the offence of the cross till you have first conciliated the respect of your hearers by a show of human learning and reasoning. And when your Master must be preached directly, don't begin at his death. Speak of his life, its benevolence, its beauty. Compare his moral precepts with those of heathen sages. Christ as the example and the teacher is your great theme.

'No', said St Paul, 'lest the cross should be of none effect, that your faith should not stand in the wisdom of men, but in the power of God.' They remembered the words of their Lord, 'I, if I be lifted up, will draw all men unto me.' Lifted up on the cross he had now been. Lifted up as Christ crucified for us, in the sight of the whole world, by the ministry of the gospel, he was next to be. Such was God's argument with sinful men.

They believed, and therefore preached. God gave the increase, and wonderful was the harvest.

✑ Christ in All His Person ✑ and Relations to Us

Thus dear brethren, we have our lesson. We must begin, as well as end, with Christ, and always abide in him for the life and power of our ministry, just as for the peace and joy of our own souls. But having thus begun, what remains? It is the revealed office of the Holy Ghost, as the Sanctifier and the Comforter, to *glorify Christ*. 'He shall glorify me', said the Lord. But how? '*He shall take of mine, and show it unto you.*' It is *our* office also, under the power of the Holy Ghost, to glorify Christ in all his Person and relations to us, and by the same method, namely, to *take of what pertains to him, and show it unto men*. Whatever pertains to him we are to show. We must expound 'in all the Scriptures the things concerning himself'. Of those things we will attempt a brief sketch and outline, but it must be only the merest outline, and that very imperfect.

We must preach Christ in regard to the glory of the Godhead which he had with the Father before the world was. We cannot exhibit the death of the cross to which he became obedient, without considering the infinite majesty of the throne from which he descended. We must keep the connection which the Apostle has given us between the glory of our Lord before he came in the flesh and his humiliation in the flesh. You remember that '*he became obedient unto death, even the death of the cross*', is introduced by '*being in the form of God, he thought it not robbery to be equal with God*' (*Phil. 2:6–8*).

In the same connection are the Incarnation and Birth of our Lord. Very near are the mysteries of Bethlehem to those of Calvary. We cannot tell how Jesus bore our sins without telling how he took our nature. To show that he *could* stand in man's place under the law, we must show that he was made very man. Hence, in the Apostle's account, between the form of God from all eternity and the obedience unto death, the connecting event is, '*he was made in the likeness of man*'. We must take care that in a just zeal for his divinity, we do not impair or put in a place of comparative unimportance his humanity.

The one is as essential to the gospel as the other – the perfect man as the perfect God. Our confession glories as much in the Word 'made flesh' as in the truth that the same Word 'was God'. In beholding and showing the great salvation, we are to consider as of equal necessity thereto 'the *Man* Christ Jesus', and that he was, and is, 'Jehovah our righteousness'. In the earliest ages of Satan's attack upon the integrity of the gospel, the heresies did not more assail the essential divinity than the real humanity of Christ, knowing that if he were not perfect man, the sacrifice for man's sins would be as unavailing as if he had been only man.

The assaults of these present times are indicative, we think, of the same strategy. How carefully and minutely do the Scriptures exhibit our Lord as man in all that is of man, while at the same time we are made to behold his glory, 'as of the only begotten of the Father, full of grace and truth'! In the fullness of time, 'God sent forth his Son, made of a woman', that in all time and to all eternity he might be 'made unto us of God', through his death, 'wisdom, and righteousness, and sanctification, and redemption'.

In setting forth our Lord's atoning death, we must keep in full view his perfect life – that suffering life between the cradle and the cross, in which his obedience to the law, completed by the endurance of its curse for us, was all wrought out. He was the Lamb *without spot,* that he might be the sacrifice all-sufficient. It was his meetness as the purchase-price of our redemption, and at the same time the pattern of the mind which must be in us to make us meet to be partakers of that redemption. Christ our example of holiness is a most important part of the setting forth of Christ as our foundation of hope. There was one hour in his life for which he came into this world (*John* 12:23 and 17:1) but every hour while he was in this world, as leading to that, exhibited the mind that was in Christ Jesus, and which must be also in us.

✿ Christ the Continuing Priest ✿

In preaching Christ crucified, let us take care that we avoid
the mistake, not infrequently made, of terminating our
representation almost entirely with the crucifixion – as if the
slaying of the sacrifice completed the *oblation* of the sacrifice;
forgetting that the office of the High Priest was to enter
within the veil with the blood of sprinkling, carrying the
sacrifice before the mercy-seat, there to appear in the presence
of God for us, and thus to 'obtain eternal redemption for us'.
'Christ crucified' is not merely Christ on the cross, but Christ
also 'on the right hand of the throne of God', as having
'endured the cross'. That throne is called 'the throne of the
Lamb' and the redeemed in heaven are represented as praising
'the Lamb *that was slain*'.

The preaching of Christ *crucified* goes necessarily into all
that Christ did and obtained for us after, and in consequence
of, his crucifixion. His resurrection, ascension and exaltation
to headship over all things, and to be a Priest forever over the
house of God, are great themes, vitally associated with what
immediately preceded them, forming the essential connection
between what was finished 'once for all' when Jesus; died, and
what is yet to be finished 'for all that come unto God by him',
now that he 'ever liveth'. We must preach Christ in his ever-
living intercession – Christ the High Priest above, with the

incense and the blood, or we leave incomplete the view of Christ crucified.

When he cried, '*It is finished*' and 'gave up the ghost', it was the slaying of the sacrifice; it was the suffering of the Lamb of God for us; it was the being 'made a curse for us' that was then finished. 'There remaineth no more sacrifice for sin', but there does remain the perpetual oblation of the one finished sacrifice. Our hope stops not at the cross, but 'entereth into that within the veil; whither the forerunner is for us entered, even Jesus, made an high priest for ever after the order of Melchisedec' (*Heb.* 6:19–20). Thither, therefore, our ministry must also enter. Too often does what in other respects is well as gospel preaching come short of that mark.

Our preaching follows Christ in his resurrection, and *perhaps* in his ascension; but do we sufficiently place before the faith of the sinner, for his prayers and his hopes to rest on, for his consolation and peace to drink of, when he strives to come unto God, Jesus as now the living, glorious Intercessor, showing in his hands the print of the nails of the sacrifice of propitiation, and bearing in his heart all the necessities of every believer? When we exhort to running the race with patience, '*looking unto Jesus*', do we sufficiently direct the eye of the hearer to Jesus, *the glorified*, in his present office and work for us? Remember that when the Apostle said, 'He is able to save to the uttermost', he added, as the essential evidence, '*seeing he ever liveth to make intercession for us*'.

I must not pass from this immediate neighbourhood of the great sacrifice without a few words about its nature. To speak of it as a sacrifice for sin in such general terms only as leave room for the most unreal, figurative, and accommodated sense, is to come far short of our duty, and of what the special tendency of error in these days demands. When we administer the Sacrament of the Lord's Supper, we 'show the Lord's *death*'. Let us take care that when we show the same in words, we do not come short of the teaching of the sacrament concerning it. The Protestant Episcopal Church interprets that teaching with studied precision, in her communion office, in reference to errors prevalent when that office was framed. She calls the sacrifice 'a full, perfect, and sufficient sacrifice, oblation, and satisfaction for the sins of the whole world'. She teaches us to pray for remission of sins *through faith in the blood* of Christ. We must imitate that precision in reference to errors now propagated. Besides the perfectness and sufficiency of the sacrifice, in opposition to those who would add to it, we must insist strongly and pointedly on its strictly *propitiatory* and *vicarious* nature, in opposition to those who would destroy it.

Under such strong texts as 'Christ hath redeemed us from the curse of the law, being made a curse for us' (*Gal.* 3:13) and 'He hath made him to be sin for us who knew no sin'

(*2 Cor.* 5:21), we must teach Christ as standing literally in our stead, under the condemnation of our sins, all our guilt laid upon him, he the condemned One for us, that we might be accounted the righteous in him. I see not how we can come short of such a sacrifice, and yet preach Christ crucified, according to the Scriptures.[1]

⁌ Christ the Teacher and King ⁍

Closely allied to our Lord's priesthood, offering the perpetual oblation of his sacrifice, is his office as the great Prophet and Teacher of his church. 'In him are hid all the treasures of wisdom and knowledge.' He is 'made unto us of God *wisdom*', as well as 'righteousness'. Christ crucified is Christ the Light as well as the Life. To his invitation, 'Come unto me and I will give you rest', is joined the precept, '*Learn of me*'. The great *subject* of saving learning is Christ himself, and he is the only effectual teacher of the learning. They that have 'learned Christ', so as truly to know him, are declared to have

---

[1] The strictly *substitutionary* character of Christ's sacrifice for our sins I consider of the most vital importance to be clearly taught if we would satisfy the language of Scripture, or do our duty to God and man. 'He was made sin for us', by which I understand that he stood for us under the law, by imputation of our sins, bearing all our sins, and as perfectly identified and charged with them as it was possible for One who 'knew no sin' in himself to be.

'*been taught by him the truth as it is in Jesus*'. Whatever our advantages of human teaching, even of the truest exposition of God's inspired Word, all is powerless spiritually to enlighten us in the knowledge of God and of Christ till he who speaks as never man spake shall add to it the teaching of his Spirit, so that we shall learn, not merely by the Scriptures, but *from* and *of him*. Christ as '*the truth*' as well as '*the way*', 'the wisdom' as well as 'the righteousness of God', the living 'Word' as well as the ever-living Priest and Intercessor, must be showed in our ministry, if we preach Christ crucified, not merely as once on the cross, but as now in his glory.

But Christ crucified is not only 'the righteousness of God' and 'the wisdom of God', but '*the power of God* unto salvation'. 'Him hath God exalted to be a *Prince*', that he may be a Saviour, '*mighty to save*'. 'Unto the Son, he saith, Thy throne, O God, is for ever and ever: a sceptre of righteousness is the sceptre of thy kingdom.' Christ as King, in a glorious sovereignty over all things in heaven and earth, we must declare. It is the crowning aspect of Christ the crucified. It is the THRONE of '*the Lamb that was slain*' before which the multitudes without number of the saved in heaven are represented as ascribing 'power, and riches, and wisdom, and strength, and glory, and honour, and blessing'. By his death he purchased, as Mediator, a glorious kingdom of redemption. At his ascension he went to receive it. There now he reigns over all else, for his people. When he shall come again, it will be in the glory of that kingdom. It was a grand introduction to that precious invitation, 'Come unto me, all ye that labour and are heavy laden', and that attending precept, 'Take my yoke, and learn of me', when he said in the verse next before, '*All things are delivered unto me of my Father*' (*Matt.* 11:27).

It was when he was in the humiliation and sufferings of the cross, that, as the great King, he stretched forth the sceptre of his power to the malefactor at his side, and gave him repentance and remission of sins, and opened unto him the kingdom of heaven. And now that, having endured the cross, he is set down at the right hand of the throne of God, to reign for ever and ever, he hath all power to make good all his promises to those who receive him, and to punish with everlasting destruction those who reject him.

There is no part of that ancient hymn of Christian praise, the *Te Deum laudamus*, that more lifts up the worship of the heart than these two sentences, 'Thou art the King of Glory, O Christ!' 'When Thou hadst overcome the sharpness of death, Thou didst open the kingdom of heaven to all believers.' It is as King of Glory, that he freely receives every sinner who seeks his salvation, writing the law of his kingdom in his heart, giving him victory over the enemies of his soul, making him triumphant in death, and finally saying unto him from his throne, 'Enter thou into the joy of thy Lord.'

It is as Christ crucified, and glorified, and 'King of Saints', that he utters that promise of royal authority and power, 'To him that overcometh will I grant to sit with me in my throne, even as I also overcame and am set down with my Father in his throne' (*Rev.* 3:21).

Here, then, is another aspect in which we must lift up the Lord Jesus in our ministry. We must not let it be forgotten that, in all the tenderness of his invitations and promises, he speaks 'as one that hath authority', not only to make them good, but to punish their rejection. The invitations of his grace are the commandments of his throne, to be answered for at his bar.

Hence the preaching of Christ crucified ceases not till it has exhibited 'the judgment-seat of Christ'. It must be noted that when the Apostle says, 'knowing *the terror of the Lord*, we persuade men', he is speaking of the terror of our Lord Jesus in his day of Judgment (*2 Cor.* 5:10–11). That day is called 'the great day of *the wrath of the Lamb*' (*Rev.* 6:17). Why the wrath of the Lamb? Why, but to keep still in view the great sacrifice of atonement. To teach that Christ on the throne of judgment is Christ that was crucified. That the chief question of that day will be, whether we have accepted or neglected the great salvation purchased by his blood; and the chief terror of that day will be the vengeance of that blood upon its rejection. While we love to speak of the blessedness of 'the saints in light' as 'joint heirs with Christ', we cannot discharge our whole duty as preachers of Christ, unless we speak of the heritage of those who 'receive his grace in vain'.

You have a most impressive example in St Paul, who, knowing nothing in his ministry 'but Jesus Christ and him crucified', pictured so solemnly that day when, coming 'to be glorified in his saints, and to be admired in all them that believe', the Lord Jesus 'shall be revealed from heaven . . . in flaming fire taking vengeance on them that . . . obey not the gospel . . . who shall be punished with everlasting destruction from the presence of the Lord, and from the glory of his power' (*2 Thess.* 1:7–9).

✄ Christ Our Inheritance For Ever ✄

But the preaching of Christ as the crucified extends through all the inheritance of his people for ever and ever. It deserves your particular remark how carefully, in many places, the Scriptures, in speaking of the actual condition of the redeemed in heaven, and its connection with the Lord Jesus as its author, source and substance, so speak of it as to keep not only Christ on the throne, but Christ *crucified*, Christ *the sacrifice*, in most conspicuous view. This is especially seen wherever he is spoken of in his Glory as '*the Lamb*', which of course means the Lamb of *sacrifice* – the antitype of the paschal lamb and of the daily sacrifice of the law; the fulfilment of Isaiah's prophecy, 'He is led as a lamb to the slaughter', 'wounded for our transgressions'. Thus the multitude which no man can number, who stand in white raiment and with palms of victory before the throne, are represented as '*before the Lamb*', and their adoration is in ascribing '*salvation to the Lamb*', and notice is carefully drawn to their having 'washed their robes in the blood of *the Lamb*', and all that high communion and blessedness is called '*the marriage-supper of the Lamb*', and in all that dwelling-place '*the Lamb is the light thereof*', and he that 'feeds them and leads them to living fountains of water' is '*the Lamb which is in the midst of the throne*', and 'the river of water of life', representing their whole felicity, proceeds '*out of the throne of the Lamb*', and the book of citizenship of the New Jerusalem, in which are written the names of all that are to inhabit there, is 'the book of life of *the Lamb slain from the foundation of the world*' (*Rev.* 13:8 and 20:12).

Most evidently the intent of all this is to carry adoring thoughts of the sacrifice of the cross into our every thought of heavenly happiness, and to represent the heir of that felicity as never forgetting that great price; never seeing the Lord in his glory without seeing him as once 'crucified and slain'; never ascending any height of 'the heavenly places', or drinking at any stream of their blessedness, without seeing in Christ not only 'the Author and the Finisher', but all in him as 'the *Lamb slain*', as he that '*liveth and was dead*', Christ the propitiation, Christ crucified. *Atonement by sacrifice* is written all over the heritage of the righteous. It is the chorus of every song of the saints in light. All heaven echoes with '*Thou wast slain, and hast redeemed us to God by thy blood'* (*Rev.* 5:9). So must it be in all our preaching concerning the happiness of the saved: Christ the Purchaser and Dispenser, but the glory of his cross never separated from the glory of his throne. When we 'shall see him as he is', we shall not cease to think of him as he was.

Here a word about our representations of the happiness of the redeemed in heaven – what constitutes it. There is a chilling effect of many books and sermons on that subject – so much generality, so little about what the Scriptures place so far above all; so much made of the subordinate and accessory features, the pastures and the flowers of the heavenly land, and so little of the Sun that gives them all their beauty and life; as if you should speak of the garden of Eden, and make more of what God planted than of the presence and communion of God therein, not remembering what Paradise in all its beauty became to man when that communion was withdrawn.

Christ is carefully to be preached as being himself, in his glory and communion, the heaven of his people; as well as, in his humiliation and sacrifice, its purchase-price. How striking is the testimony of the Scriptures to this point! Has Jesus gone away to prepare a place for us in his Father's house? His promise is, 'I will come again, and receive you unto myself, that where I am there ye may be also.' Does he pray his Father on behalf of the happiness of his people? The prayer is, 'that they may be with me where I am, and behold my glory'. While it doth not appear what we shall be as 'sons of God' and 'joint-heirs with Christ', St John speaks of one thing that we do know. It is that 'we shall be like him', and 'see him as he is'. Does Jesus promise, to them that overcome, that they 'shall eat of the hidden manna'? That manna is himself. 'I am that bread of life.' Is heaven described as a glorious city of habitation? 'The Lamb is the temple', and 'the light thereof'. Has it a river of water of life, and on either side of it the tree of life? All that river comes forth from 'the throne of the Lamb'. Christ is 'the Finisher of our faith' in this, that he is, in himself, the consummation of our hope; his presence, his communion, his everlasting love being the prize of our high calling, and the goal of our race. We come to him now, and he is our peace. We go to be with him for ever, and he is our glory. Ask the way to heaven, we say, *Christ*. Ask where heaven is, we say, *where Christ is*. Ask what heaven is, we answer, *what Christ is*. Thus we preach Christ crucified whenever we speak according to the Scriptures of what constitutes the life eternal of the sinner, 'redeemed by the blood of the Lamb'.

᜕ Christ Ever Present ᜒ

But we must take good heed that we do not speak of our Lord in his heavenly power and glory so as not to give due place to his ever-present ministry, in and to his Church on earth. The impression is too prevalent that here, in our duties, and wants, and prayers, we have only a Saviour and Helper afar off.

The precious assurance of the Scriptures is, that we have a Saviour so near to every one of us that he is 'a very present help' – so present that nothing can separate us from him; that nothing but unbelief ever intervenes between our wants and his fullness, neither space nor time, nor unworthiness nor weakness – so present that he is ever at the door, waiting to be received, or beneath our weakness, ready to be leaned on. No presence is so '*very* present' as that of the ever-living Christ, in the power of his Spirit to every heart that seeks him – enlightening, guiding, comforting, upholding, drawing sinners to himself, making himself known to them, giving efficacy to means of grace; whatever the instruments, he the only power. 'I am the Good Shepherd.' All is comprehended in that declaration. As the Good Shepherd, he is the *present* Shepherd; so present to each of the flock, that he 'calleth every one by name, and leadeth him out'. Oh, what a help and comfort it is when we get a full comprehension and an abiding impression of *that living, loving, all-powerful presence!* How it strengthens the minister of the gospel! How it lifts up the heart of the Christian!

In this connection, the faithful preaching of Christ will keep in great prominence that aspect of himself which he so much emphasized when he spoke of himself as '*the living bread – the bread of God'*, of whom the manna in the wilderness was the type, and the bread of our Eucharist is the Sacrament; Christ the present daily life of his people; they abiding in him by faith, he in them by his Spirit; all their life as children of God now, all their hopes of life for ever, depending on that habitual communion – the vine and the branches. The more we ourselves enjoy of that *abiding*, the better shall we know how to teach it. Nowhere does mere book-knowledge of what is given us to preach assist us less.

When we speak of Christ as *'the life'*, fulfilling the type of the manna, let us take care that we set in clear view, not only our dependence, but his *freeness*. It was one prominent aspect of that 'spiritual meat', of which 'all our fathers' of the church in the wilderness ate, that all classes and conditions of people partook of it alike, and all with equal and perfect freeness. It lay all around the camp, as accessible to one as another. Neither Moses, nor Aaron, nor any priest or ruler, had any privilege at that table which the humblest Israelite had not. The priesthood had no office of intervention between the hungry and that bread. *Whosoever will, let him take and eat*, was the proclamation. Let us take good heed that what we cannot deny in the type be not narrowed or concealed in the Antitype. Our text is, *'Him that cometh to me, I will in no wise cast out'* (*John* 6:37). And I do not know a text that contains more of the essence of the preaching of Christ in the richness and freeness of his salvation. Oh, let us take care that our ministry shall keep full in the sight of men that open way, that free access, that directness of coming, not to some mere symbolical representation, but to the *very present* Christ, in all his tenderness of love and power to save.

Ordinances, ministers, are sadly out of place, no matter how divinely appointed for certain uses, when, instead of mere helps in coming to Christ, they are made, in any sense, conditions or terms of approach, so that the sinner gets to Christ only, or in any degree, by them. The light of the sun is not more free to every man that cometh into the world than is the salvation of Jesus to every believing sinner. It is our business to be continually showing that precious truth; coming by faith, the sole condition – Christ, the full and perfect salvation of all that come.

4

⌒⊙⊙⌒

TRUTHS CONNECTED WITH PREACHING CHRIST

B ut in the range of gospel truth there are subjects of instruction which, though not directly concerning Christ's Person and office, are so connected with all right appreciation of his saving grace that we cannot keep them out of view without affecting most injuriously our whole ministry. Be it remembered that while the cross, with its immediate neighbourhood, is the metropolis of Christianity, all the region round about is Holy Land, more or less holy according to the nearness to that 'city of our God'; 'a land of milk and honey', 'of brooks and fountains of water', intersected in all directions with highways by which pilgrims to Zion approach the desire of their hearts. It is the office of the gospel preacher to map out that land; to trace those converging roads; to set up the way-marks to the City of Refuge.

Christ is not fully preached when any truth which teaches the sinner's need of such a Saviour, illustrating his preciousness by showing our ruin and beggary through sin dwelling in us, and bringing condemnation upon us, is kept in obscurity. The wisdom of 'the scribe instructed unto the kingdom of heaven' to 'bring forth out of his treasure things new and old', is found in his omitting nothing connected with the gospel, however remote from the great central truths and duties; and in his giving to each its portion in due season, as well as its place in due relation.

⁓ Conviction of Sin ⁓

Christ is our '*righteousness*' unto justification to every one that believeth so that in him there is no condemnation (*Rom.* 8:1). But we shall preach him in vain, in that light, unless we show the sinner's absolute need of such righteousness. We must seek, under the power of the Holy Ghost, so to convince him of sin that he shall see himself to be under the condemnation of God's law, without excuse and without hope, till he flies to that refuge. Blessed is he whose ministry the Spirit employs to teach that lesson of ruin and beggary. It is the threshold of the way of life.

The textbook in that teaching is the law — God's will, as our rule of life, however and wherever expressed. Preached in a spiritual application to the secrets of the heart, not only as the rule of obedience but as the condition of peace with God to every one that is *not* in Christ Jesus, and on the perfect keeping of which all his hope depends, preached in view of the salvation of Jesus as only increasing the condemnation so long as it is salvation neglected, it is the instrument of the Holy Ghost to strip the sinner of self-reliance and self-justification, to humble him before God under a sense of guilt and ruin, and as a 'schoolmaster to lead him to Christ, that he may be justified by faith'.

He that would preach a full justification in Christ, *without* works, must preach entire condemnation under the law, *by* works. By the law is the knowledge of sin, and hence the knowledge, in part, of Christ. Clear, unequivocal statements of the divine law; the full exhibition of the text, '*Cursed is every one that continueth not in all things written in the book of the law to do them*' (that continueth not in all things from first to last of life), thus carrying the sword of the Spirit into the discerning of the thoughts and intents of the heart, is the special basis of, and preparation for, all saving knowledge of Christ. The way of the Lord is prepared by that forerunner. How many more consciences would cry out for relief under the load of sin, how much oftener would the careless heart be awakened to seek mercy through Christ, were there only a more searching comparison of all that is in man with all the holiness of the will of God!

Again, Christ is 'made unto us *sanctification*' (*I Cor.* 1:30). But how can we do justice to so cardinal a truth of God's grace, unless we do ample justice to that other great truth of man's nature, out of which arises all the need of a Sanctifier — the entire 'corruption of the nature of every man that is naturally engendered of the offspring of Adam' (*Article* 9 of the Protestant Episcopal Church)? The beginning of sanctification is to be born again of the Holy Ghost. As are men's views of the extent to which by nature they are corrupt and alienated from God, so will be their views of the spiritual nature, necessity, and extent of that great change. Hence, to preach Christ in sanctification, we must preach man in his natural corruption. The '*carnal mind*' is '*enmity against God*', and is '*not subject to the law of God, neither indeed can be*' (*Rom.* 8:7). Let us faithfully expound those words of St Paul. We need no stronger declaration as the basis of the whole superstructure of the need of an entire inward regeneration, making the sinner a new creature in Christ Jesus — new in heart, new in life and hope. That this preaching of the necessity of such a new creature is eminently the preaching of Christ, we have a striking testimony in these words of the Epistle to the Ephesians (4: 20–24): 'Ye have not so learned Christ; if so be that ye have heard him, and have been taught by him, as the truth is in Jesus: that ye put off . . . the old man, which is corrupt according to the deceitful lusts; and be renewed in the spirit of your mind; and that ye put on the new man, which after God is created in righteousness and true holiness.'

๛ Dependence on the ๑ Holy Spirit

But how shall we speak of so great a spiritual transformation without speaking with equal stress of him who produces it? What sanctification is to salvation, such is the right teaching of the power and office of the Holy Ghost, the Sanctifier, the Spirit of Christ, and all-comprehending gift of God.

What is there in the Christian life, from first to last, that is not the work of the Holy Ghost? Is the sinner convinced of sin? Jesus sent the Spirit to do that work. Is he quickened from spiritual death? *'It is the Spirit that quickeneth.'* Is he born again? He is *'born of the Spirit'*. Is he spiritually-minded? It is because he *'minds the things of the Spirit'*. Is he a *'follower of God'*, as a dear child? It is because he is *'led by the Spirit of God'*. Has he an internal evidence of that sonship? It is because *'the Spirit beareth witness with his spirit'*. Is the love of God *'shed abroad in our hearts'*? It is *'by the Holy Ghost given unto us'*. Do we learn how to pray as we ought? It is because '*the Spirit helpeth our infirmities*'. Are we comforted with the consolation of Christ? The Spirit is '*the Comforter*'. Are we strengthened in our duty? It is '*by his Spirit in the inner man*'. Do we grow in the knowledge of Christ? Jesus said of the Holy Ghost, '*He shall take of mine and show it unto you.*' And, besides the spiritual resurrection and sanctification, will these vile bodies also rise? Will they also be sanctified and made glorious according to the glory of our risen Lord? It is written, 'He shall quicken your mortal bodies by his Spirit that dwelleth in you' (*Rom.* 8:11).

Rightly to honour the Holy Ghost as he is thus revealed in his own inspired Word – how important to the faithfulness and fruitfulness of our ministry! We may so come short of it, we may so contradict it that, while bearing a very reputable character before men, we may all the while be 'grieving the Holy Ghost', yea, even 'resisting the Holy Ghost'.

How much barrenness in the work of the ministry in making, not mere church-members, but spiritually-enlightened and spiritually-minded followers of Christ, may be ascribed to deficiency – negativeness at least – in this great department of our teaching! In no part of his work does a minister more need to be taught of God, or to sit humbly at the feet of Jesus to learn of him; nowhere does a decline of spirituality of mind so soon show itself as here.

In no part of our work do we depend more upon a decided, habitual, personal experience in our own souls of God's gracious operation. It is here that great departures from the truth, which go on to carry away eventually whole communities of professing Christians into manifold and essential errors, almost always secretly or overtly begin; as it is the final construction of a system from which the personal office of the Holy Ghost is virtually, if not professedly, excluded, in which they culminate.

The scriptural description of a spiritual mind is that it 'minds the things of the Spirit'. It is equally the test of a spiritual and evangelical ministry. That which specially tries our spiritual discernment and skill in rightly dividing the word of truth is the right adjustment of means of grace in their relation to the power of grace, of instruments of blessing to the hand that employs them and that gives them all their efficacy. The Spirit has his instruments. His grace has its means. His great instrument in our sanctification is his own revealed truth, by which he testifies and glorifies the Lord Jesus in our eyes. Sacraments are that same essential truth, taught under other signs, and sealed with a special impressiveness.

The preaching of that same truth by an ordained ministry is the great instrumentality of the Spirit. The point of caution is, while giving all due place to the instrument, that we keep it exclusively in the place of a mere instrument

— of no avail in itself; that we treat it as we treat the glass by which we seek to see some distant star — not as an object to be looked at, but only as a help to look immeasurably beyond and above it; that as the glass is nothing without the light, so the means of grace are nothing without 'the Spirit of grace'; that all the power is of the Holy Ghost, and *that* power not deposited in the means, as we put bread into the hand of a distributor, so that whosoever receives the latter receives the bread. That power is never divorced from the personal ministry of the Spirit, but applied directly by himself to each heart that receives his grace, he 'dividing to every man severally as he will'.

To speak of an ordinance, a sacrament, any means of grace, even the Holy Scriptures of truth, as if they were in any sense the power unto salvation, or as if they contained, whatever its original source, the grace by which we live unto God, thus leading men to look to them, instead of only, by their help, to Christ and his Spirit is to 'do despite to the Spirit of grace'.

The whole truth in this connection is found where the Apostle says, 'Who is Paul, and who is Apollos, but ministers by whom ye believed, *even as the Lord gave to every man*' (*I Cor.* 3:5). Instead of Paul and Apollos, read any ordinance or means of grace. What are they but ministrations of man by the help of which ye believe, even as the Lord giveth to every man?

✑ A Crucial Text ✑

There is a text which the full and explicit preaching of Christ will be always directly or indirectly, consciously or unconsciously, illustrating. It is those verses in the second chapter of the Epistle to the Ephesians, 'By grace are ye saved, through faith; and that not of yourselves: it is the gift of God: not of works, lest any man should boast. For we are his workmanship, created in Christ Jesus unto good works.'

Salvation is all of grace alone; in its origin in the love of God; in its purchase by the blood of Christ; in the first quickening of the sinner from the death of sin; in all the renewal of his nature; in his acceptance through Christ to the peace of God; in his whole ability to live as a child of God; and in his final admission to the glory; of God – *all of grace only* – wonderful grace! But it is *through faith alone,* and that faith itself a gift of grace; our works in every degree and aspect wholly excluded from the work of saving us, though necessarily included *as fruits* of the grace that does save us – we being created anew in Christ Jesus unto good works, and not in any degree *by* good works.

First comes God's workmanship, making us new creatures, then our working as so created 'unto good works which God hath ordained that we should walk in them'.

We preach such works, first, as absolutely excluded, from having any part in procuring our justification before God;

secondly, as essential fruits and evidences of our having obtained such justification. We preach the office of faith as so vital that only by it are we united to Christ, as living stones built upon the living head of the corner (*I Pet.* 2:5–7); and the necessity of good works as so absolute that only in them can we walk as God has ordained, and have evidence that we are true believers in Jesus; and at the same time we preach both faith and works as deriving all their being from the Spirit of God, and all value and efficacy to salvation from the righteousness of Christ.

✺ The Whole Counsel of God ✺

Here let me add some few miscellaneous observations. We are bound to instruct the believer in all the privileges and consolations that are in Christ, that his joy may be full. But we must lay equal stress on all his obligations, that Christ may be glorified. Out of the same wounds of the cross come privilege and duty, promise and commandment, the consolation of faith and the duty of obedience; and the same preaching that leads to the one must alike insist on the other, and on both as necessary to our having that rest which Jesus promises.

It is a great matter so to preach the precepts of Christ as to lead men to embrace his promises; and so the promises as to draw the disobedient to the love of his precepts. In all our work we have two great sources of persuasion, according to the example of St Paul, namely, 'We beseech you by *the mercies* of God' and again, 'Knowing *the terror of the Lord*, we persuade men'; the love of God in Christ as a Saviour, and the wrath of God in Christ as Judge of quick and dead; a cloud of light and a cloud of darkness, each proceeding from the cross as accepted or rejected.

We must do all in tenderness, but all in faithfulness. The whole counsel of God embraces the fearful penalty of unpardoned sin as well as the glorious inheritance of the reconciled in Christ. The faithful preacher of Christ keeps back none of it. While he delights in the loving aspects of his grace, he is not ashamed of the severities of his justice. He does not, indeed, denounce or judge. It is not for him to commend or condemn. His work is always to entreat and persuade; tenderly, lovingly, patiently, in the mind of Christ. But persuasion has the alarming truths to use as well as the encouraging.

That '*God is a consuming fire*' out of Christ is as much an argument of persuasion and tenderness as that, in Christ, 'God is Love'. We read of '*the goodness and severity of God*' (*Rom.* 11:22). We must exhibit both. They interpret and enforce one another. But how to balance aright judgment and mercy, invitation and warning, precepts of obedience and promises of consolation, the tender '*Come unto me, and I will give you rest*', with the stern '*Depart, ye* cursed, into everlasting fire;' the darkness and the light – the loving voice from the mercy-seat and the dreadful sentence from the Judgment-seat – all under the duty of teaching and preaching Jesus Christ, is not learned from books only and is not given by specific rule. It comes chiefly out of the state of the heart, under the general light of the Scriptures, and by a careful endeavour to learn of, and be like, him of whom it is beautifully written, that he hath 'the tongue of the learned, to know how to speak a word in season to him that is weary' (*Isa.* 50:4).

From all that has now been said, it appears how mistaken is the idea that by confining our preaching to Christ and him crucified we have a very narrow range of truth to expatiate in. In reality, we have the whole vast range of natural and revealed religion. A wider field no preacher can find who does not seek it beyond the confines of religious truth.

The difference between the man who confines himself to the preaching of Christ, and him who does not, need not be that the latter embraces any portion of divine truth – of doctrine or duty, of history or prophecy or precept, which enters not into the range of the former. It may be wholly a difference in the mode of presenting precisely the same truth – a difference in the bearings, in the relations assigned to every part; in the cardinal points to which all is adjusted; in the *polarity,* so to speak, which governs such manifestation of truth as deserves the name and praise of the preaching of Christ. You may take truth from the immediate neighbourhood of the cross, or from the farthest boundaries of the domain of Christianity, and, when its just relation to Christ and his redemption is exhibited, Christ is preached. Thus there is no reason why, in the most faithful ministry, there may not be abundant variety of topic and of instruction. The sermon may be always shining in the light of our glorious Lord, while receiving it either by direct looking unto him, or indirectly from secondary objects, which, as satellites of the sun, revolve around him and shine in his glory. The sermon, in all its spirit and tendency, may say, *'Behold the Lamb of God'*, and yet the view may be as changing as the positions from which it is taken, the circumstances which influence it, the lights and shadows of the several conditions and necessities of the minds before which it is placed.

In general, we may say, that as no subject is legitimate in the preaching of a minister of Christ that does not admit of being presented in some important relation to Christ, so no sermon is evangelical that does not truly exhibit such relation, giving him the same position to the whole discourse that he holds in the Scriptures to the whole body of truth therein. As some subjects have a much nearer and more vital relation to him than others, they will be much the most frequent and engrossing in the preaching of a faithful

Christian minister. The great truths, the great facts, the great duties and privileges and interests and consolations which proceed the most directly from the Person and office, the death and intercession of Christ, and the work of the Holy Spirit, as well as those which lead the most immediately thereto, will be so habitually the subjects of his preaching that the more remote and indirect will be only occasional exceptions to the standing rule and habit. And which of these classes of subjects his mind and heart most delight in, and which draws forth the deepest earnestness and the strongest emotions of his soul, will not be doubtful.

I have now exhibited as much of this great and wide subject as I could, with any propriety, occupy your time with. You will, of course, understand that I have not attempted to embrace the whole field. What has been attempted, I am deeply conscious, is most imperfect and inadequate. Still I have not withheld my best endeavours where even St Paul exclaimed, '*Who is sufficient for these things!*'

5

⌒⊙⊙⌒

QUALIFICATIONS
FOR PREACHING
CHRIST

I conclude with a brief view of the state of mind and
spirit which qualifies a minister to be a faithful preacher of
Christ. The first qualification is a spirit of faith.

✑ A Spirit of Faith ✑

I mean faith, not merely in such of its exercises as make the
minister a living Christian, and a growing, vigorous Christian,
but in that special exercise which enables him to go on

patiently, persistently, hopefully, immovably, preaching the gospel as we have seen the Apostles preached it, in like simplicity and spirituality – with as little of the devices and mixtures and dilutions and subterfuges of man's wisdom, no matter what the obstacles or what the apparent fruitlessness – believing it is God's own way, to which alone his blessing is promised, and, which he *will* bless as his own 'wisdom and power unto salvation'.

It was precisely with such meaning that St Paul, just after he had pronounced, 'We preach not ourselves, but Christ Jesus the Lord', and just after he had adverted to the fact that such preaching failed to open the eyes of many that heard, saying 'If our gospel be hid, it is hid to them that are lost, in whom the god of this world hath blinded the minds of them which believe not' (*2 Cor.* 4:3–4) – it was in full view of all whom their preaching did not succeed in convincing, but only made the more hardened and hopeless, that he said, '*We believe, and therefore* speak' (*2 Cor.* 4:13), meaning not only that they believed what they spoke, but that they believed it was just what God commanded them to speak, and they realized its unspeakable importance and preciousness to the souls of men. And no rejection of it by man could shake that confidence, or lead them to speak anything else, or in any other way. Well they knew what a 'stumbling-block to the Jew', and what utter 'foolishness to the Greek', was their testimony concerning Christ crucified;

but not a word would they change – '*We believe, and therefore speak.*'

It was this lesson of faith that Paul gave to Timothy. He warned him of a time of apostasy approaching. 'The time will come when they will not endure sound doctrine; . . . and they shall turn away their ears from the truth, and shall be turned unto fables' (*2 Tim*. 4:3–4). How then was Timothy to act in such times? What '*sound doctrine*' meant in the mind of St Paul, we well know – all that way of justification by the righteousness of Christ imputed, and of sanctification by the Spirit of God imparted, to the believer; that whole way of life, of which the *vicarious* propitiation by the sacrifice of Christ was the central power and life. It was all that doctrine which men would not endure.

And what was Timothy to do? Was he to conclude that he, and other preachers of Christ, had taken the wrong method because it was thus unsuccessful? That they must find out some other sort of preaching because that was so rejected? Since men would not endure sound doctrine, must they try to get them into the church, or if in the church already, to make them satisfied to stay there by giving them unsound doctrine? If the truth caused the carnal mind's enmity against God to turn away from it, must *they* turn away from the truth, and give them another gospel? What said the faith of an apostle? No compromise – no accommodation – only so much more earnestly and continually to preach that same rejected doctrine. Hear Paul's remedy! 'I charge thee therefore before God, and the Lord Jesus Christ, who shall judge the quick and the dead at his appearing and his kingdom; preach the word; [the same offensive word], be instant in season, out of season; reprove, rebuke, exhort with all longsuffering and doctrine' (*2 Tim.* 4:1–2). The more the truth is turned away from, so much the more proclaim it. God will see to the issue. 'So we speak, not as pleasing men, but God, which trieth our hearts.' Such is the faith of which we are speaking, as of such importance in our ministry.

The *times* which St Paul predicted, and which began before Timothy had ended his labours, are yet in being. We all know how they have been exhibited since the beginning of the nineteenth century, both in this country and in Europe, under the form of Unitarianism and Rationalism. It is the old demand: 'The Greeks seek after wisdom.' And we must meet it with the old satisfaction: '*We preach Christ crucified*, unto the Jews a stumblingblock, and unto the Greeks foolishness; but unto them which are called, both Jews and Greeks, Christ the power of God, and the wisdom of God' (*I Cor.* 1:22–24)

The *atonement* is the great offence – that one perfect and sufficient oblation and satisfaction for sin, in the death and sacrifice of our Lord Jesus Christ, perfect God and perfect man in the unity of his divine Person, and in the bearing of our iniquities; being 'made a curse for us' under the sentence of the law, of which our sin is the transgression – *that* atonement embraced and made availing to each man's salvation through a living faith, and equally accessible and efficacious to all that do thus believe in the Lord Jesus, whether the wise or the unwise, the great or the despised, the chief of sinners or those much less sinful, so that in this respect there is no difference, because 'all have sinned'.

That atonement, with all the branches of truth and duty, of privilege and responsibility, which reside in it and depend on it, and which lose all place and life and value the moment that True Vine is taken away – *that* is the offence. *That* is the 'sound doctrine' which the wisdom of this world cannot endure; for which it labours to find a substitute, and to get rid of which the inspiration of the Scriptures is so fought against, lest men should be obliged to take them as a final Rule of Faith and Life.

Now when this is the case, what course must a faithful minister of Christ adopt? I ask the question to illustrate the faith of which I am speaking: '*We believe, and therefore speak.*' Must we, *may* we preach *the Word,* as Paul understood and preached it, one whit the less plainly, simply, boldly, with more of the enticing words of man's wisdom, in order the more to please men, and in that degree the less to approve ourselves unto God whose messengers we are, and whose message we have no permission to change, to dilute, to interpolate, or to conceal?

Shall we suppose that to preach Christ, as the Apostles did, is not as much now, and as exclusively, 'the wisdom and power of God', as it was when they preached? Or shall we *believe* as they believed, and therefore *speak* as they spoke, to all people, and with all perseverance, and prayer, and boldness, though the whole earth be drowned in unbelief, and men everywhere be turned unto fables? What is the answer of a true faith in God? No change, no dilution, no compromise – no *progress* but in the line of the more close following of the Apostles, in spirit, in faith, in purity, in simplicity.

The old exhortation still sounds aloud through the church, and will to the end – 'Preach the Word', the same old Word – instant in season, and *so* 'do the work of an evangelist, and make full proof of thy ministry'. If the time has come when men will not endure that Word, and will turn away from that truth, the time will come to every faithful, patient, earnest, loving, believing minister thereof when the hearts of the disobedient shall, under the power of God, be turned unto the wisdom of the just, and they that sat in darkness and spiritual death, without hope, shall come to the light of life in Christ Jesus, and being made new creatures in him, shall count all things but loss for the excellency of the knowledge of his great salvation (*2 Tim.* 4:2–5).

Let patience have her perfect work. Be not faithless, but believing. God's hand is not shortened that it cannot save by that same Word now as in the ancient times.

✍ A Spirit of Love ✍

But to preach Christ is not only 'a work of faith', it is 'a labour of love'. I will not say that no man can do it in a certain sense, that is, with doctrinal correctness, without the love of Christ in his heart; for St Paul speaks of some in his day who preached Christ, 'even of envy and strife, not sincerely', from selfish and evil motives. I will not prolong this address in enlarging on the elementary truth, that without a personal experience of the preciousness of Christ to our own souls, by each one's individual participation in the hope that rests on his justifying righteousness, and is witnessed by the sanctifying power of his Spirit dwelling in us, we cannot preach Christ, according to his will, in his mind, in the tenderness, and earnestness, and patience, and godly wisdom, which alone become his ministry, however correct our teaching in a mere doctrinal aspect.

What I wish in these concluding words to insist on is the importance of a very earnest, tender, and overcoming love, to give living religion to our theology, and the mind of Christ to our teachings concerning him. Two preachers, alike in accurate and full statement of all that is revealed concerning our blessed Lord and his salvation, may be very different in the spiritual power of their ministry, and the difference will not depend so much on the superiority of talent or of eloquence, or even of diligence in one over the other, as on their comparison in point of love.

He will preach best who loves most. His preaching will go most to the heart, and will be attended with most of the 'demonstration of the Spirit' who, in all he says and does, is most constrained by the love of Christ, dictating, animating, sanctifying, with the tenderness and patient earnestness of his Master's mind, his whole discourse. Oh, that we were more earnest to grow in this grace! What ought we to value in personal attainment compared with it? If you shall attain to the ministry, and find it fail in spiritual efficacy, inquire into the cause, by searching the state of your hearts in regard to the love of Christ therein, to what extent the aim, the zeal, the topics, the temper of your work, and the whole character of your personal example, are under the dominion of that love.

But I have already occupied too much of your time, and yet I feel that I have come very far short of the height and breadth of what I have sought to exhibit. 'We have this treasure in earthen vessels, that the excellency of the power may be of God and not of us.' Blessed be God that in our weakness we have his power to lean on. I humbly pray that power of God to bless to you, my dear brother, what in so much weakness, and imperfectness, and unworthiness I have now addressed to you. Nothing in this world could I rejoice in so much as to be instrumental, under God's grace, in promoting the spiritual excellency and efficacy of your future work and your personal growth in the faith and love of Christ. The time is at hand when nothing else will seem of the smallest value. I commend you to God, and to the word of his grace, which is able to build you up, and make you good stewards of the unsearchable riches of Christ.

'Now the God of peace, that brought again from the dead our Lord Jesus, that great Shepherd of the sheep, through the blood of the everlasting covenant, make you perfect in every good work to do his will, working in you that which is well pleasing in his sight, through Jesus Christ; to whom be glory for ever and ever. Amen.'

Such is the prayer of your friend and brother in the gospel of Christ,

CHARLES PETTIT MCILVAINE

Appendix:

The Subject of Apostolic Preaching

cĐŌ©ᐯ

C. H. Spurgeon[1]

'And daily in the temple, and in every house, they ceased not to teach and preach Jesus Christ' (*Acts* 5:42).

I do not know whether there are any persons here present who can contrive to put themselves into my present position and feel my present feelings. If they can effect that, they will give me credit for meaning what I say when I declare that I feel totally unable to preach. And, indeed, I think I shall scarcely attempt a sermon, but rather give a sort of declaration of the truths from which future sermons shall be made. I will give you bullion rather

[1] The first sermon preached in the Metropolitan Tabernacle, London, 25 March 1861. Sermon No. 369 in the *Metropolitan Tabernacle Pulpit, 1861* (London: Passmore & Alabaster), p. 169.

than coin. The block from the quarry and not the statue from the chisel.

It appears that the one subject upon which men preached in the apostolic age was *Jesus Christ*. The tendency of man, if left alone, is continually to go further and further from God, and the Church of God itself is no exception to the general rule. For the first few years, during and after the apostolic era, Christ Jesus was preached, but gradually the Church departed from the central point and began rather to preach ceremonials and church offices rather than the Person of their Lord. So has it been in these modern times – we also have fallen into the same error, at least to a degree, and have gone from preaching Christ to preaching doctrines about Christ, inferences which may be drawn from his life, or definitions which may be gathered from his discourses. We are not content to stand like angels in the Sun – our fancies disturb our rest and must needs fly on the sun-beams, further and further from the glorious source of light.

In the days of Paul it was not difficult at once, in one word, to give the sum and substance of the current theology. It was Christ Jesus. Had you asked any one of those disciples what he believed, he would have replied, 'I believe Christ.' If you had requested him to show you his Body of Divinity, he would have pointed upward reminding you that divinity never had but one body, the suffering and crucified human frame of Jesus Christ who ascended up on high. To them Christ was not a notion refined, but unsubstantial – not an historical personage who had left only the savour of his character behind but whose person was dead. To them he was not a set of ideas, not a creed, nor an incarnation of an abstract theory, but he was a Person. One whom some of them had seen, whose hands they had handled – no, One of whose flesh they had all been made to eat, and of whose blood they had spiritually been made to drink. Christ was Substance to them. I fear he is too often but shadow to us. He was a reality to their minds. To us, though, perhaps, we would scarcely allow it in so many words, rather a myth than a man; rather a person who was, than he who was, and is, and is to come – the Almighty.

I would propose (and Oh! may the Lord grant us grace to carry out that proposition from which no Christian can dissent), I would propose that the subject of the ministry of this house, as long as this platform shall stand and as long as this house shall be frequented by worshippers, shall be the Person of Jesus Christ. I am never ashamed to avow myself a Calvinist, although I claim to be rather a Calvinist according to Calvin, than after the modern debased fashion. I do not hesitate to take the name of Baptist. You have there [pointing to the baptistery] substantial evidence that I am not ashamed of that ordinance of our Lord Jesus Christ. But if I am asked to say what is my creed I think I must reply, 'It is Jesus Christ.' My venerable predecessor, Dr Gill, has left a body of divinity admirable and excellent in its way. But the body of divinity to which I would pin and bind myself forever, God helping me, is not his system of divinity or any other human treatise, but Christ Jesus, who is the Sum and Substance of the Gospel. Who is in himself all theology – the incarnation of every precious Truth – the all-glorious personal embodiment of the Way, the Truth and the Life. This afternoon I will try to describe the SUBJECT, CHRIST JESUS. Secondly, to speak for a little while upon its COMPREHENSIVENESS. Then to enlarge upon its EXCELLENCIES. And conclude by testing its POWER.

I. First, then, the SUBJECT: They continued both to teach and preach *Jesus Christ*.

C. H. Spurgeon on Acts 5:42

To preach Jesus Christ aright we must preach him in his *infinite and indisputable Godhead.* We may be attacked by philosophers, who will either make him no God at all, or one constituted temporarily and, I must add, absurdly a God for a season. We shall have at once upon us those who view Christ as a Prophet, as a great man, as an admirable exemplar. We shall be assailed on all sides by those who choose rather to draw their divinity from their own addled brains than from the simplicity of Holy Writ. But what matters this? We must reiterate again and again the absolute and proper deity of Christ, for without this we are in the position of those described by the prophet, 'Thy tacklings are loosed; they could not well strengthen their mast', and soon will our enemies prevail against us and the prey of a great spoil shall be taken. Take away the divinity of Christ from the gospel, and you have nothing whatever left upon which the anxious soul can rest. Remove the Word who was in the beginning with God, and who was God, and the Jachin and Boaz of the temple are overturned. Without a divine Saviour your Gospel is a rope of sand, a bubble; a something less substantial than a dream. If Christ were not God, he was the basest of impostors. He is either one of two things – very God of very God, or else an arch-deceiver of the souls of men, for he made many of them believe he was God, and brought upon himself the consequences of what they called blasphemy. If he were not God, he was the greatest deceiver that ever lived. But God he is; and here, in this house, we must and will adore him. With the multitude of his redeemed we *will* sing

> Jesus is worthy to receive
> Honour and power *divine;*
> And blessings more than we can give
> Be *Lord* for ever thine.

To preach Christ, however, we must also preach *his true humanity.* We must never make him to be less manlike because he was perfectly divine. I love that hymn of Hart which begins

> A man there is — a real man,
> Who once on Calvary died.

'*Real* man!' I think we do not often realize that manhood of Christ. We do not see that he was bone of our bone and flesh of our flesh; feeling, thinking, acting, suffering, doing just like ourselves — one of our fellows and only above us because he is 'exalted with the oil of gladness above his fellows.' We must have a human Christ and we must have one of real flesh and blood, too; not of shadows or filmy fancies. We must have one to whom we can talk, one with whom we can walk, one

> Who in his measure feels afresh
> What every member bears,

who is so intimately connected with us in ties of blood that he is as with us one, the head of the family, first-born among many Brethren. I am never more glad than when I am preaching a *personal* Christ. A doctrinal Christ, a practical Christ or an experimental Christ, as some good men make him to be according to the temper of their minds, I do not feel to be sufficient for the people of God. We want a *personal* Christ. This has been a power to the Romish church — a power which they have used for ill, but always a power; they have had a personal Christ, but then it has either been a baby Christ in his mother's arms, or else a dead Christ upon the cross. They never reached the force of a real full-grown Christ, one who not only lived and suffered, but who died and rose again and sits at the right hand of God, the Head of the Church, the one ruler of men. Oh! we must bring out more and more clearly each day the real personality of the Redeemer in his complex Person. Whatever we fail to preach, we must preach *him*. If we are wrong in many points, if we are but right here, this will save our ministry from the flames; but if we are wrong here, however orthodox we may pretend to be, we cannot be right in the rest unless we think rightly of him.

But, further, to preach Christ Jesus it is absolutely necessary we should preach him as *the only mediator between God and man*. Admitting the efficacy of the intercession of living saints for sinners, never for a moment denying that every man is bound to make supplication for all ranks and conditions of men, yet must we have it that the only mediator in the heavens, and the only direct intercessor with God, is the man Christ Jesus. Nay, we must not be content with making him the only mediator; we must set aside all approach to God in any way whatever, except by him.

We must not only have him for the priest, but we must have him for the altar, the victim and the offerer too. We must learn in full the meaning of that precious text, 'Christ is all'. We must not see a part of the types here and a part there, but all gathered up in him, the one door of heaven, the one crimson way by which our souls approach to God. We must not allow that approaches can be made in human strength, by human learning, or by human effort; but in him and through him, and by him, and in dependence upon him, must all be done between God and man. We have no wings, my brethren, with which to fly to heaven; our journey there must be on the rounds of Jacob's ladder. We cannot approach God by anything we have, or know, or do. Christ crucified, and he alone, must lift us up to God.

And more, we must preach Christ in the solitariness of his redemption work. We must not permit for a moment the fair white linen of his righteousness to be stained by the patch-work of our filthy rags. We must not submit that the precious blood of his veins should be diluted by any offering of ours co-acting therewith for our salvation. He hath, by one sacrifice, for ever put away sin. We shall never preach Christ unless we have a real atonement. There are certain people nowadays who are making the atonement, first a sort of compromise, and the next step is to make the atonement a display of what ought to have been, instead of the thing which should have been. Then, next, there are some who make it to be a mere picture, an exhibition, a shadow – a shadow, the substance of which they have not seen. And the day will come, and there are sundry traces of it here and there, in which in some churches the atonement shall be utterly denied, and yet men shall call themselves Christians, while they have broken themselves against the cornerstone of the entire system. I have no kith nor kin nor friendship, nor Christian amity, with any man whatever who claims to be a Christian and yet denies the atonement.

There is a limit to the charity of Christians and there can be none whatever entertained to the man who is dishonest enough to occupy a Christian pulpit and to deny Christ. It is only in the Christian church that such a thing can be tolerated. I appeal to you. Was there ever known a Buddhist acknowledged in the temple of Buddha who denied the basic doctrine of the sect? Was there ever known a Mohammedan Imam who was sanctioned in the mosque while he cried down the Prophet? It remains for Christian churches only to have in their midst men who can bear the name of Christian, who can even venture to be Christian teachers, while they slander the Deity of him who is the Christian's God and speak lightly of the efficacy of *his* blood who is the Christian's atonement. May this deadly cancer be cut out root and branch; and whatever tearing of the flesh there may be, better cut it out with a jagged knife than suffer it to exist, because no lancet is to be found to do it daintily. We must have, then, Christ in the efficacy of his precious blood as the only Redeemer of the souls of men, and as the only mediator, who, without assistance of ours, has brought us to God and made reconciliation through his blood.

Our ministry will scarcely be complete unless we preach *Christ as the only Lawgiver and Rabbi of the church.* When you put it down as a canon of your faith that the church has right and power to decree rites and ceremonies, you have robbed Christ at once of his proper position as the only teacher of the church. Or when you claim the office of controlling other men's consciences by the decree of the church, or the vote of a synod, apart from the authority of Christ, you have taken away from Christ that chair which he occupies in the Christian church as the teacher in the great Christian school, as the Rabbi, and the only Rabbi, of our faith. God forbid that we should hold a single truth except on his authority. Let not our faith stand in the wisdom of man, but in the power of God. You refer me to the writings of Doctor this and Doctor the other: what are these? The words of Christ, these are truth, and these are wisdom. You bring the authority from the practice of a church three or four centuries removed from the crucifixion as the proof of the existence of a certain ceremony and the righteousness of certain ecclesiastical offices. What is your proof worth? If Christ has not specially ordained it, and if he has not commanded his people to obey it, of what value is any rite whatever? We acknowledge Christ as ordaining all things for his church and presenting that church with a finished code of laws, from which any deviation is a sin, and to which any addition is a high crime. Any church officer who is not ordained of Christ occupies an office which he ought to resign. Any person who practises a ceremony for which he has not scriptural authority should renounce it; and any man who preaches a doctrine for which he has not Christ as his certifier, should not demand for it the faith of men.

But I fear there are times coming when the minister will not be true to his duty unless he goes further and preaches Christ as *the sole King of the church*. There has been a disposition on the part of the state, especially with regard to the Free Church of Scotland, to exercise power and judgment over church decrees. No king, no queen that ever lived, or can live, has any authority whatever over the church of Christ. The church has none to govern and rule over her but her Lord and her King. The church can suffer, but she cannot yield; you may break her confessors alive upon the wheel, but she, in her uprightness, will neither bend nor bow. From the sentence of our church there is no appeal whatever on earth.

To the court of Heaven a man may appeal if the sentence of the church is wrong, but to Caesar never. Neither the best nor the worst of kings or queens may ever dare to put their finger upon the prerogative of Christ as the head of the church. Up, church of God! If once there are any laws of man passed to govern thee, up, dash them in pieces! Let us each catch up the war cry, and uplift the lion standard of the tribe of Judah; let us challenge the kings of the earth and say, 'Who shall rouse him up?' The church is queen above all queens, and Christ her only King. None have jurisdiction or power in the church of Christ save Jesus Christ himself. If any of our acts violate the civil laws, we are men and citizens and we acknowledge the right of a state to govern us as individuals. None of us wish to be less subjects of the realm because we are kings and priests unto God. But as members of Christian churches we maintain that the excommunication of a Christian church can never be reversed by the civil power, or by any state act, nor are its censures to be examined, much less to be removed, mitigated, or even judged. We must have, as Christ's church, a full recognition of his imperial rights, and the day will come when the state will not only tolerate us as a mere society, but admit that as we profess to be the church of Christ, we have a right by that very fact to be self-governing and never to be interfered with in any sense whatever, so far as our ecclesiastical affairs are concerned.

Christ must be preached and exalted in all these respects, or else we have not preached a full Christ; but I go one step further. We have not yet mounted to the full height of our ministry unless we learn to preach *Christ as the King of kings*. He has an absolute right to the entire dominion of this world. The Christian minister, as ordained of God to preach, has a perfect right in God's name to preach upon any subject touching the Lord's kingdom, and to rebuke and exhort even the greatest of men. Sometimes I have heard it said, when we have canvassed the acts of an emperor or senator, 'These are politics.' But Christ is King of politics as well as theology. 'Oh! but', say they, 'what have you to do with what the State does?' Why, just this: Christ is the head of all states, and while the state has no authority over the church, yet Christ himself is King of kings and Lord of lords. Oh, that the church would put her diadem upon her head and take her right position! We are not slaves. The church of God is not a grovelling corporation bound forever to sit upon a dunghill; never queen was so fair as she, and never robe so rich as the purple which she wears. Arise, O church! arise – the earth is thine; claim it. Send out thy missionary, not as a petitioner to creep at the feet of princes, but as an ambassador for God to make peace between God and man. Send him out to claim the possession which belongs to thee, and which God has given to thee to be thine for ever and ever, by a right which kings may dispute, but which one day every one of them shall acknowledge.

The fact is, we must bring *Christ himself* back into camp once more. It is of little use having our true Jerusalem swords, and the shields, and the banners, and the trumpets, and the drums; we want the King himself in the midst of us. More and more of a personal Christ is the great lack of the time. I would not wish for less doctrine, less experience, or less practice, but more of all this put into Christ, and Christ preached as the sum and substance of it all.

2. But, secondly, I am now to speak, for a short time, upon the COMPREHENSIVENESS OF THE SUBJECT which the text announces.

It is an old and trite saying that the ministers of the gospel may be divided into three kinds – the doctrinal, the experimental and the practical. The saying is so often repeated that very few would contradict it. But it betrays at once, if it be true, the absence and lack of a something essentially necessary for the church's success. Where is the preacher of *Christ* out of these? I propound this, that if a man be found a preacher of Christ, he is doctrinal, experimental, and practical. The *doctrinal* preacher generally has a limited range. He is useful, exceedingly useful; God constitutes him a barrier against the innovations of the times: he preaches upon his subjects so frequently that he is well versed in them, and becomes one of the armed men about the bed of Solomon. But suppose the doctrinal preacher should have it all his own way, and there should be none others at all, what would be the effect? See it in our Baptist churches about one hundred and fifty years ago. They were all *sound* and sound asleep. Those doctrines had preached them into a lethargy, and had it not been for some few who started up and proposed the missions for the heathen, and who found but little sympathy at first, the church would have been utterly inactive. Now, I would not be hard with any, but there are some brethren still whose preaching might justly be summed up as being doctrinal, nothing more than doctrinal, and what is the effect of their ministry? Bitterness. They learn to contend not only earnestly for the faith, but savagely for it. Certainly, we admire their earnestness, and we thank God for their soundness. But we wish there were mingled with their doctrine a somewhat else which might tone down their severity and make them seek rather the unity and fellowship of the saints than the division and discord which they labour to create.

Again, I will refer you to the next class of preachers, the *experimental*. How delightful it is to sit under an experimental preacher! Perhaps of all ministries this one is the most useful – he who preaches the doubts, the fears, the joys, the ecstasies of the people of God. How often do the saints see the footsteps of the flock, and then they find the shepherd under an experimental minister! But do you know the effect of an experimental minister, purely so, I mean, when all else is put aside to make room for experience? There is one school of divines always preaching the corruption of the human heart. This is their style:

'Except thou be flayed alive by the law; except thou art daily feeling the utter rottenness of thine heart; except thou art a stranger to full assurance, and dost always doubt and fear; except thou abidest on the dunghill and dost scrape thyself with a potsherd, thou art no child of God.'

Who told you that? This has been the preaching of some experimental preachers, and the effect has been just this. Men have come to think the deformities of God's people to be their beauty. They are like certain courtiers of the reign of Richard III, who is said by history to have had a hump upon his back, and his admirers stuffed their backs that they might have a graceful hump, too. And there are many who, because a minister preaches of doubts and fears, feel they must doubt and fear, too; and then that which is both uncomfortable to themselves and dishonouring to God comes to be the very mark of God's people. This is the tendency of experimental preaching, however judiciously managed, when ministers harp on that string and on that alone: the tendency is either to preach the people into a soft and savoury state, in which there is not a bit of manliness or might, or else into that dead and rotten state in which corruption outswells communion and the savour is not the perfume of the king's ointments, but the stench of a corrupt and filthy heart.

Take also the *practical* preacher; who would say a word against this good man? He stirs the people up, excites the children of God to holy duties, promotes every excellent object, and is in his way an admirable supplement to the two other kinds of ministers. But sit under the practical preacher; sit under him all the year round and listen to his people as they come out. There is one who says, *'The same thing over again – Do, do, do, nothing but do.'* There is a poor sinner yonder just gone down the front steps. Follow him. 'Oh,' says he, 'I came here to find out what Christ could do for me, and I have only been told what *I* must do for myself.' Now this is a great evil, and persons who sit under such a ministry become lean, starveling things. I would that practical preachers would listen to our farmers, who always say it is better to put the whip in the manger than upon the horse's back. Let them feed the people with food convenient for them, and they will be practical enough; but all practice and no promise, all exhortation and no sound doctrine, will never make the man of God perfect and zealous for good works.

But what am I driving at in bringing up these three sorts of ministers? Why, just this: to show you that there is one minister who can preach all this, without the dangers of any one of the others, but with the excellencies of the whole. And who is he? Why, any man in the world who preaches Christ. If he preaches Christ's Person he must preach *doctrine.* If I preach Christ I must preach him as the Covenant Head of his people and how far am I then from the doctrine of election? If I preach Christ I must preach the efficacy of his blood and how far am I removed then from the great doctrine of an effectual atonement? If I preach Christ I *must* preach the love of his heart, and how can I deny the final perseverance of the saints? If I preach the Lord Jesus as the great Head and King, how far am I removed from divine Sovereignty? Must I not, if I preach Christ personally, preach his doctrines? I believe they are nothing but the natural outgrowth of that great root thought, or root substance rather, the person of the Lord Jesus Christ. He who will preach Christ fully will never be lax in doctrine.

And what better *experience* can you preach than in preaching Christ? Would you preach the sufferings of the saints, preach *his* agony and bloody sweat, his cross and passion; for the true sufferings of the saints are in fellowship with him. If you would preach their joys, preach *his* resurrection, his ascension and his advent. You are never far from the joys of the saints when you are near to the joys of Christ; for did not he say that his joy should be in them, that their joy might be full?

And what better *practice* can be preached than preaching Christ? Of every virtue he is the pattern; of the perfection of human character, he is the very mirror; of everything that is holy and of good report, he is the abiding incarnation. He cannot fail, then, to be a good doctrinal, experimental, practical preacher who preaches Christ. Did you ever know a congregation grow less spiritual by a minister preaching Christ? Did you ever know them get full of doubts and fears by preaching Christ? Did you ever hear of their getting lax in sentiment by his preaching Christ? Did you ever hear a whisper that men became unholy in their lives because they heard too much about Christ? I think that all the excellencies of all ministers may be gathered up into the teaching of the man who can preach Christ every day in the week, while there will not be any of the evils connected with the other forms of preaching.

3. I shall now pass on to notice some of the surpassing EXCELLENCIES of the subject.

First, he will always have *a blessed variety* in his preaching. In Australia I have heard that the only change for the backwoodsmen is to have one day damper, tea and bread; the next day, bread, damper and tea; and the next day, tea, bread and damper. The only variety some ministers give, is one Sunday to have depravity, election, and perseverance and the next Sunday, election, perseverance, and depravity. There are many strings to the harp of the gospel. There are some brethren who are so rightly charmed with five of the strings, which certainly have very rich music in them, that they never meddle with any of the other strings; cobwebs hang on the rest, while these five are pretty well worn out. It is always pretty much the same thing from the first of January to the last of December. Their organ has very few keys, and upon these they may make a very blessed variety, but I think not a very extensive one. Any man who preaches Christ will ensure variety in his preaching. *He* is all manner of precious perfume, myrrh, and aloes, and cassia. He is all sorts of music, he is everything that is sweet to the ear; he is all manner of fruits; there is not none dainty in him but many. This tree of life bears twelve manner of fruits. He is all manner of raiment; he is golden raiment for beauty; he is the warm raiment for comfort; he is the stout raiment for harness in the day of battle. There are all things in Christ, and he that hath Christ will have as great a variety as there is to be found in the scenery of the world where are no two rocks alike, and no two rivers wind in precisely the same manner, and no two trees grow in precisely the same form. Any other subject you may preach upon till your hearers feel satiety; but with Christ for a subject, you may go on and on and on, till the sermon swells into the eternal song, and you begin to sing, 'Unto him that loved us and washed us from our sins in his own blood.'

There is yet another excellence about this subject, namely, that *it suits all sorts of people.* Are there rebels present? Preach Christ; it will suit them. Are there pardoned sinners present? What is better to melt their hearts than the blood of the Lord Jesus? Are there doubting Christians? What can cheer them better than the name of Christ? Are there strong believers? What is stronger meat than Jesus crucified? Are there learned, polite, intellectual hearers? If they are not satisfied with Christ, they ought to be. Are there poor, ignorant, unlettered men? Jesus Christ is just the thing to preach to them – a naked Christ to their simple ears. Jesus Christ is a topic that will keep in all climates. Land in New Zealand in the midst of uncivilized men, move off to another post and stand in the midst of poetical Persia or fickle France, the cross is adapted to all. We need not inquire into the doctrinal opinion of our hearers. If they are high, I am sure Christ will suit them. If they are low, if they be true believers, I am sure Christ Jesus will suit *them.* No Christians will reject such meat as this; only prepare it and with a hot heart serve it up on the table, and they will be satisfied and feed to the full. So that there is adaptation as well as variety in this subject.

4. But more than this, I must add, and this will bring me to my last point, for my time flies, there is a POWER about this subject when it is preached with the demonstration of the Spirit, which is not found in any other. My brethren, what power there is in this subject to promote *the union* of the people of God! There is a man there, he is almost a Puseyite. 'I do not like him', says one. Stop till I tell you something more about him, and you will. There is another man there, a Presbyterian – true blue. He cannot bear Independency, or anything but Presbytery – a covenant man. 'Well,' says one, 'I like him a little better; but I do not suppose we shall get on very well.' Stop! I will tell you some more about him. There is another man down there; he is a very strong Calvinist. 'Humph,' says one, 'I shall not admire *him*.' Stop, stop! Now, here are these three men; let us hear what they say of each other. If they know nothing of each other except what I have stated, the first time they meet there will be a magnificent quarrel. There is yonder clergyman – he will have little fraternity whatever with the ultra-Evangelical; while the Presbyterian will reject them both, for he abhors black prelacy. But, my dear brethren, all three of you, we of this congregation will approve of you all, and you will approve of one another when I have stated your true character.

That man yonder, whom I called almost a Puseyite, was George Herbert. How he loved the doornails of the church! I think he would scarce have had a spider killed that had once crept across the church aisles. He was a thorough churchman, to the very centre of the marrow of his bones; but what a Christian! What a lover of his sweet Lord Jesus! You know that hymn of his which I have so often quoted and mean to quote a hundred times more – 'How sweetly doth my Master's sound', and so forth. I hear a knock at the door. 'Who is that?' 'Why, it is a very strong churchman.' 'Do not show him in; I am at prayer; I cannot pray with him.' 'Oh, but it is George Herbert!' 'Oh, let him in, let him in! No man could I pray better with than Mr Herbert. Walk in, Mr Herbert. We are right glad to see you. You are our dear companion; your hymns have made us glad.'

But who was that second man, the Presbyterian, who would not have liked George Herbert at all? Why, that was Samuel Rutherford. What a seraphic spirit! What splendid metaphors he uses about his sweet Lord Jesus! He has written all Solomon's Song over without knowing it. He felt and proved it to be divine. The Spirit in him re-dictated the song. Well now, I think, we will introduce Mr Rutherford and Mr Herbert together and I am persuaded when they begin to speak about their Master they will find each other next of kin. And I feel sure that, by this time, Samuel Rutherford and George Herbert have found each other out in heaven, and are sitting side by side.

Well, but then we mentioned another; who was that high Calvinist? He was the man who was called the Leviathan of Antinomians. That he was a leviathan I will grant, but that he was an Antinomian is false. It was Dr Hawker. Now, I am sure George Herbert would not have liked Dr Hawker and I am certain that Dr Hawker would not have liked George Herbert, and I do not suppose that Samuel Rutherford would have had anything to do with either of them. 'No, no,' he would say, 'your black prelacy I hate.' But look at Hawker, there is a sweet spirit; he cannot take up his pen but he dips it in Christ, and begins to write about his Lord at once. 'Precious Immanuel – precious Jesus.' Those words in his morning and evening portions are repeated again and again and again. I recollect hearing of Mr Rowland Hill, that he said to a young man who was at tea with him one night when he was about to go: 'Where are you going to?' 'Oh!' said he, 'I am going to hear Dr Hawker, at St George's in the Borough.' 'Oh, go and hear him,' he said; 'he is a right good man, worth hearing. But there is this difference between him and me; my preaching is something like a pudding, with here and there a plum. But Dr Hawker's is all plum.' And that was very near the mark, because Dr Hawker was all Christ. He was constantly preaching of his Master; and even if he gave an invitation to a sinner, it was generally put in this way: 'What sayest thou? Wilt thou go with *this man*, and be married and espoused unto *him*? It was the preaching of a personal Christ that made his ministry so full of marrow and fatness.

My dear friends, let a man stand up and exalt Christ, and we are all agreed. I see before me this afternoon members of all Christian denominations; but if Christ Jesus is not the topic that suits you, why then I think we may question your Christianity. The more Christ is preached, the more will the church prove and exhibit and assert and maintain her unity. But the less Christ is preached, and the more of Paul, and Apollos, and Cephas, the more of strife and division and the less of true Christian fellowship.

We will only mention the power of the preaching of Christ *upon the heart of sinners*. There is a person, now a member of my church, whose conversion was owing to the reading of that hymn,

Jesus, lover of my soul.

'Ah,' said he, 'does Jesus love my soul? Then how vile I have been to neglect him.' There are scores whose conversion is distinctly and directly traceable, not to doctrine – though that is often useful – nor experience, nor practice, though these are fruitful, but to the preaching of Christ. I think you will find the most fertile sermons have always been the most Christly sermons. This is a seed which seldom rots under the clod. One may fall upon the stony ground, but it more often happens that the seed breaks the stone when it falls, and as Christ is a root out of a dry ground, so this finds root for itself even in dry, hard, stony hearts. We ought to preach the law, we ought to thunder out the threatenings of God, but they must never be the main topic. Christ, Christ, Christ, if we would have men converted.

Do you want to convince yonder careless one? Tell him the story of the cross. Under God it will arrest his attention and awaken his thoughts. Would you subdue the carnal affections of yonder profligate? Preach the love of Christ, and that new love shall uproot the old. Would you bind up yonder broken heart? Bring forth Christ, for in him there is a cordial for every fear. Christ is preached and we do rejoice, yea, and will rejoice, for he is 'the power of God unto salvation unto everyone that believeth'.

Judge not, my dear brethren, any man's ministry. The world has too often condemned the man whom God intended to honour. Say not of such a one, 'He can do no good, for his language is rough and rude.' Say not of another that his style is too often marred with flippancy. Say not of a third that he is too erudite or soars too high. Every man in his own order. If that man preach Christ, whether he be Paul, or Apollos, or Cephas, we wish him God speed; for God will bless the Christ he preaches and forgive the error which mingled with his ministry. I must even frankly admit the truth of many a criticism that has been uttered on my ministry, but I know it has been successful, and under God it has been, because I *have* sought to preach Christ. I say that without boasting or egotism, because if I had not done so, I had no right to be a minister of

Christ at all, and as I claim to be God's minister, I will and must declare it, whatever I have not preached, *I have preached Christ*, and into whatsoever mistakes I have fallen, I have sought to point to his cross, and say, 'Behold the way to God.' And if you see others preaching Christ, be not you their foe. Pray for them; bear them in your arms before God; their errors may yet be outgrown, if they preach Christ; but if not, I care not what their excellency may be, the excellency shall die and expire like sparks that go out in darkness. They have not the fuel of the flame, for they have not Christ Jesus as the substance of their ministry.

May I entreat, in closing, your earnest prayer, each one of you, that in this house as well as in all the places of worship round about, Christ may evermore be preached, and I may add my own sincere desire that this place may become a hissing and the abode of dragons and this pulpit be burned with fire, if ever any other gospel be preached here than that which we have received of the holy apostles of God, and of which Jesus Christ himself is the chief corner stone. Let me have your incessant prayers. May God speed every minister of Christ. But where there is so large a field of labour, may I claim your earnest and constant intercessions that, where Christ is lifted up, men may be drawn to hear, and afterwards drawn to believe, that they may find Christ, the Saviour of our souls. 'He that believeth and is baptized shall be saved; but he that believeth not shall be damned.' 'Repent and be converted, every one of you,' said Peter. Yet again, said Paul to the jailer, 'Believe on the Lord Jesus Christ, and thou shalt be saved, and thy house.'

God give us grace to believe, and unto him
be glory for ever and ever.
Amen.